HOUGHTON MIFFLIN

Friends

INVITATIONS
TO LITERACY

Houghton Mifflin Company • Boston

Atlanta • Dallas • Geneva, Illinois • Palo Alto • Princeton

HOUGHTON MIFFLIN

Friends

Senior Authors

J. David Cooper
John J. Pikulski

Authors

Kathryn H. Au
Margarita Calderón
Jacqueline C. Comas
Marjorie Y. Lipson
J. Sabrina Mims
Susan E. Page
Sheila W. Valencia
MaryEllen Vogt

Consultants

Dolores Malcolm
Tina Saldivar
Shane Templeton

INVITATIONS
TO LITERACY

Houghton Mifflin Company • Boston

Atlanta • Dallas • Geneva, Illinois • Palo Alto • Princeton

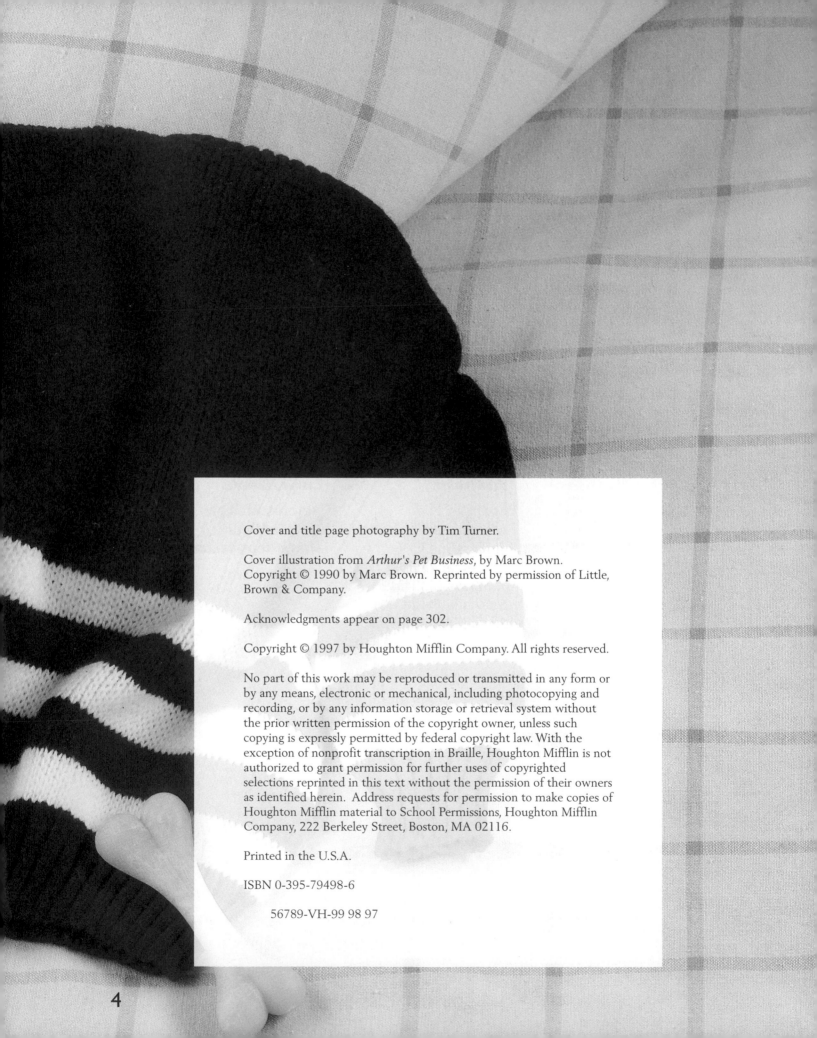

Cover and title page photography by Tim Turner.

Cover illustration from *Arthur's Pet Business*, by Marc Brown.
Copyright © 1990 by Marc Brown. Reprinted by permission of Little,
Brown & Company.

Acknowledgments appear on page 302.

Printed in the U.S.A.

ISBN 0-395-79498-6

56789-VH-99 98 97

BIG BOOK PLUS

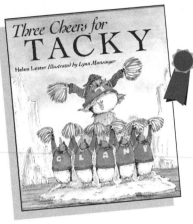

Getting Started

Three Cheers for Tacky

a story
by Helen Lester
illustrated by Lynn Munsinger

Watch that lovable penguin, Tacky, as he leads his team in a cheering contest.

Themes

CONTENTS

PET SHOW TODAY!

CONTENTS

BE A NATURE DETECTIVE

Good Friends

PET SHOW

TODAY !

13

BIG BOOK PLUS

The Cats of Tiffany Street
by Sarah Hayes

Table of Contents

WATCH **ME** READ

Family
Fleas

WATCH **ME** READ

A Pet
for Scat

WATCH **ME** READ

Wendy's
Puppy

HENRY AND MUDGE
AND THE
Happy Cat
Story by Cynthia Rylant
Pictures by Suçie Stevenson

PAPERBACK **PLUS**

More Books You Can Read!

Ask Marc Brown

**Marc Brown with his
daughter, Eliza**

*Did you ever have a pet business when you
were a boy?*

One summer a friend and I decided to invent a
new product that dogs might love. We called it Dog
Pudding. We put all sorts of things into a giant pot.
We cooked this mess. It was the most disgusting
slop I had ever seen, but we thought dogs might like
it. We got a couple of neighborhood dogs ready to
taste the pudding. The dogs wouldn't go near it.
So we were stuck with five tons of dog pudding.

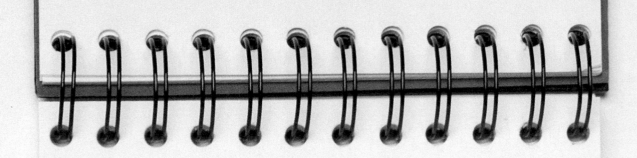

Why is Arthur an aardvark?

Arthur started as a bedtime story. My son Tolon wanted me to tell him a story about an unusual animal. "Aardvark" popped up. Then he wanted to know what the aardvark's name was. I picked a name that started with the letter *a*, as in *aardvark*. That's how Arthur was born.

Marc Brown with his wife, daughter, and their cat Teddy

recent
tail
injury

← This is Athena.
she is 80 in cat years.

← This is Teddy.
She is 8 in cat years.

This is where
I work.

This is where
my wife,
Laurie, works. →

These are our studios in the barn
where we make our books.

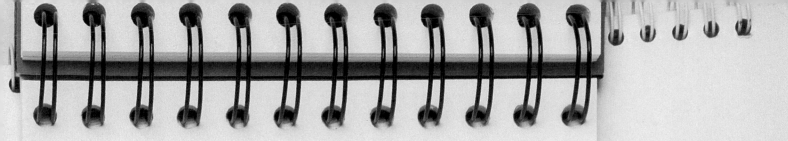

Where do you get ideas for your stories?

My stories all start from things that happen to people in real life. I think that's where the funniest and best ideas are.

I don't just sit down and write a story and expect that it will turn out perfectly the first time. Usually each story is rewritten as many as thirty times before I'm happy with the way it sounds.

How did you first become interested in storytelling?

My great-grandmother and grandmother told my sisters and me stories all the time. Sometimes we would ask for a spooky story. Grandma Thora would tell us a spooky story, but first she would take out her false teeth. That made the story *really* spooky!

19

MARC BROWN

ARTHUR'S
PET BUSINESS

ANT FARM

PEA[...]

AN ARTHUR ADVENTURE

"You've been looking at puppies for months," said D.W. "When are you going to ask Mom and Dad if you can have one?"

"I'm waiting for just the right moment," said Arthur, "so promise not to say anything!"

That night at dinner, Father asked,
"What's new?"
"Arthur wants a puppy," said D.W.
"Blabbermouth!" said Arthur.

"A puppy is a big responsibility," said Father.

"I can take care of it," said Arthur.

"We'll think about it," Mother said.

"That means no," explained D.W.

After dinner Mother and Father did the dishes.

"Can you hear what they're saying?" asked
Arthur.

"They're worried about the new carpet,"
whispered D.W.

Suddenly the door opened.

"We've decided you may have a puppy if you can take care of it," said Father.

"Wow!" said Arthur.

"*But*," said Mother, "first you need to show us you're responsible."

"How will I ever prove I'm responsible?" asked Arthur.

"The best way I know is to get a job," said D.W. "Then you can pay back the seven dollars you owe me!"

"Ka-chingg!" went her cash register.

26

Arthur wondered what
kind of job he could do.
    "You could work for my
dad at the bank," said Muffy.
"He needs some new tellers."

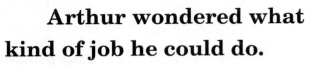

"If I were you, I'd get a job
at Joe's Junk Yard crushing old
cars," offered Binky Barnes.

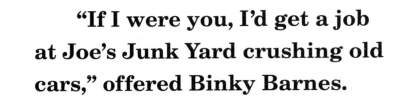

"Do something that *you* like,"
said Francine.
    That gave Arthur an idea.

27

"I'll take care of other people's pets,"
said Arthur, "then Mom and Dad will know
I can take care of my own."

Arthur and Francine put up signs to
advertise his new business.

His family helped, too.

Arthur waited and waited. Then, just before bedtime, the phone rang.

"Hello," he said. "Arthur's Pet Business. How may I help you?

"Yes. No. When? Where? Great!" said Arthur.

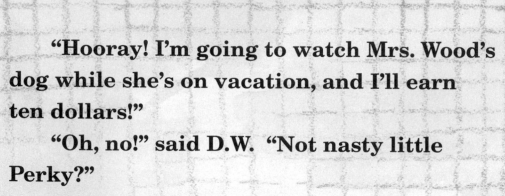

"Hooray! I'm going to watch Mrs. Wood's dog while she's on vacation, and I'll earn ten dollars!"

"Oh, no!" said D.W. "Not nasty little Perky?"

"Isn't that the dog the mailman calls 'JAWS'?" asked Father.

"That's Perky!" said D.W.

31

The next morning, Arthur ran all the
way to Mrs. Wood's house.
"Right on time!" said Mrs. Wood.
"*Grrrrr,*" growled Perky.

"She hasn't been herself lately," said Mrs. Wood. "I'm worried."

"I'll take good care of her," said Arthur. "We'll be best friends."

"*Grrrrr*," growled Perky.

"Here's her schedule and a list of things she doesn't like," said Mrs. Wood. "I'll see you next Sunday."

33

Arthur did his best to make Perky feel at home. Every day he brushed her. He tried to fix her favorite foods. They took lots of long walks — day and night.

Perky made sure they had the whole sidewalk to themselves.

"You look exhausted," said Mother.
"Maybe taking care of a dog is too much
work . . ."

"Any dog I get will
be easier than Perky,"
said Arthur.

35

Word of Arthur's pet business got around. On Monday the MacMillans asked Arthur to watch their canary, Sunny.

On Tuesday Prunella gave Arthur her ant farm.

On Wednesday the Brain asked Arthur to take care of his frogs while he went on vacation.

Best of all, on Thursday The Amazing
Larry asked Arthur to keep Cuddles, his
trained boa constrictor.

Animals were everywhere —
until Mother put her foot down.
"I want all these animals in the
basement *now*!" she ordered.

38

By bedtime all the pets were downstairs. All except Perky. Perky slept in Arthur's room.

On Saturday Buster asked Arthur to go to the movies.

"I can't," said Arthur. "When I finish cleaning these cages, it will be feeding time.

"And anyway, it's Perky's last night with me and she seems sick. I don't want to leave her."

"Well, I bet you're happy today," said D.W. the next morning. "You get rid of Perky and collect ten dollars!"

"I can't believe it," said Arthur. "But I'm going to miss Perky."

"Arthur, Mrs. Wood just called to say she's on her way over," said Mother.

"Now, wait here, Perky," ordered Arthur. "I'll go and get your leash."

When Arthur went back into the kitchen, Perky was gone.

"Here Perky! Perky!" called Arthur. But Perky didn't come.

"She's not in the basement," called Father.

"She's not in the backyard," said D.W.

"She's lost!" said Arthur.

"Oh, oh!" said D.W. "You're in big trouble!"

"Arthur, Mrs. Wood is here!" called Mother.

"Hi, Mrs. Wood," said D.W. "Guess what? Arthur lost Perky!"

"My poor little darling is lost?" asked Mrs. Wood.

"Don't worry," said Father. "Arthur's looking for her right now."

Suddenly they heard a bark.

"Everybody come quick!" called Arthur.

"Look," said Arthur. "Perky's had puppies!"

"No wonder she's been acting so strange," said Mrs. Wood.

"You've done a wonderful job taking care of Perky, when she needed a friend the most. How can I ever thank you?"

48

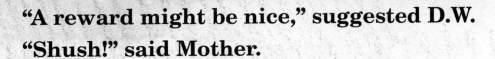

"A reward might be nice," suggested D.W.

"Shush!" said Mother.

"Here's the money I owe you," said Mrs. Wood. "And, how would you like to keep one of Perky's puppies as a special thank you?"

"I'd love to," said Arthur. "If I'm allowed."

"Of course," said Mother. "You've earned it."

"Wow!" said Arthur. "Ten dollars *and* my very own puppy! I can't believe it!"

"Neither can I," said D.W. "Now you can finally pay back my seven dollars."

"Ka-chingg!" went her cash register.

Pets Wanted

Arthur put up signs to advertise his pet business. Think about how you could help Arthur advertise. Work alone or with a partner. Choose a way to share your ideas.

- **Make a poster.**
- **Write a radio ad.**

Include in Your Ad

$ what it will cost

Arthur's phone number

the kinds of pets Arthur takes care of

Arthur's Pet Business

51

Snoopy's Adventure

A Story by Kymbrly Ray

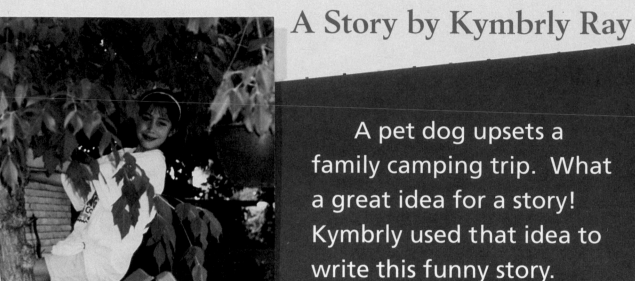

A pet dog upsets a family camping trip. What a great idea for a story! Kymbrly used that idea to write this funny story.

Kymbrly Ray
Valley View Elementary
Las Cruces, New Mexico

Kymbrly was in the second grade when she wrote this story.
Kymbrly likes pets. She has three rats, three cats, and a dog named Zipper! She also likes Mexican food, math, and the color blue.

Snoopy's Adventure

One summer day Blaze went camping at the Gila River with her mother, her brother Joe, and their pet dog, Snoopy. Snoopy was 13 years old. The river was cool and refreshing. Blaze, Joe, her mom, and Snoopy went swimming all afternoon. For dinner they cooked hamburgers and roasted marshmallows, and Snoopy ate the food, too. Then they all went to sleep.

At 4:00 A.M. Blaze's mom woke up and couldn't find Snoopy. She woke up Blaze and Joe. They looked and looked. Everyone was crying. Finally, Snoopy came back — soaking wet. She had been swimming. Blaze's mom was so happy to see her. She gave Snoopy lots of kisses and then grounded her for a week, but Snoopy is still a very spoiled dog.

AMAZING PETS!

SCUBA DOG

KidCity

IT'S SHOW TIME!

Summer is the time when just about everybody wants to jump into the water. Especially Shadow, the scuba-diving dog!

No, this is no joke. Dwane Folsom, the dog's owner, noticed his pet would follow him anywhere. (That's why he named her *Shadow*.) Dwane began taking Shadow along for company on his diving trips. One afternoon, to his surprise, Shadow jumped into the water following his air bubbles.

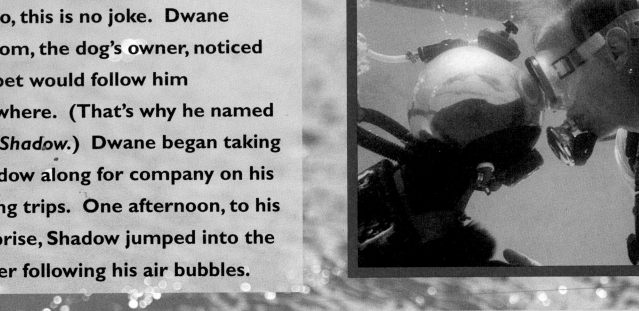

Dwane decided to try to teach Shadow to scuba dive. He invented a little plastic helmet for her. He fastened her oxygen hose to his own air tank.

At first, Shadow kept trying to take the helmet off. But after a few days of food rewards for keeping it on, Shadow was ready to go underwater.

Now, almost one year later, Shadow dives up to twenty feet deep in the ocean. She can stay underwater for almost 30 minutes. Dwane has even taken Shadow scuba diving with him to the Caribbean. **Hot dog!**

AMAZING PETS!
PARROT SAVES FAMILY

by Eve Nagler

One cold winter day the Ascolillo family found a parrot half-frozen outside their home in Massachusetts. They took the parrot inside and cared for it. Eddie and Michael Ascolillo named the parrot Elliot.

Elliot had a cage but liked to fly around the house. Elliot was friendly with the Ascolillo family, but he never made a sound.

Early one morning, almost a year later, the Ascolillo family was sound asleep. Suddenly a loud noise echoed through the house.

Mr. and Mrs. Ascolillo opened their eyes. It was Elliot! The parrot was screaming and flapping its wings over their bed!

All at once, Mr. and Mrs. Ascolillo smelled something

terrible. The smell was coming from a gas leak. The gas could kill them.

Quickly Mr. and Mrs. Ascolillo got up. They grabbed their sons, Eddie and Michael, from their beds and hurried outside. Then Mr. Ascolillo ran back into the house and rescued Elliot.

A few minutes later, the heating system in the cellar blew up. Elliot had awakened the family just in time!

An animal protection group heard how Elliot had saved the Ascolillo family. The group gave Elliot a gold medal for being a hero!

ELLIOT the HERO

Parrot honored for saving family

BOSTON (AP) — A parrot credited with saving the lives of a family when gas leaked into their home was the Animal He

Parrot Wins 1988 Animal Hero Award

A parrot named Eliott received the MSPCA's 1988 Animal Hero Award as the MSPCA honored outstanding humans and animals at its second annual Humane Awards Ceremony in May at Boston's Westin Hotel.

The parrot saved th

neighbor's dog who also attended the awards dinner. Dzekevich respo d to the cries of Wolley and had locked

Narrow Escape

A Massachusetts family spotted a parrot outside! They knew he needed their help. Parrots belong in the jungle, not in Massachusetts.

The parrot had been someone's pet, but now he was lost. His feet were frozen to a blanket. The family saved the parrot. They named him Elliott.

Maybe you heard about Elliott. He became a hero. There was a gas leak in the family's house one night. A gas leak can kill people. Elliott screamed and woke up the family just in time. Everyone got outside safely.

All Parrots Aren't So Lucky

Elliott's story had a happy ending. Most "pet" parrot stories don't.

sold in pet stores are caught in

You can help. Don't buy parrots that come from the jungle. Save Elliott's jungle friends!

Elliott's story almost ended sadly.

Parrot, dog are honored at MSCPA celebration

By Susan Zinno
Contributing Reporter

On Wednesday night, a parrot and a dog were the guests of honor at the 120th anniversary celebration of the Massachusetts Society for the Prevention of Cruelty to Animals at the Westin Hotel.

Elliot, an Amazon parrot found in a dumpster by an East Boston family on Christmas Eve six years ago, was the recipient of the 1988 Animal Hero award. The blue-chested parrot's squawking one night awakened the Ascolillo family in time to evacuate their house and escape toxic fumes from a neighborhood gas leak.

Louise Meyer of Carlisle and her German shepherd, Bonnie, were named volunteers of the year. Meyer and her dog spend much of their time visiting patients with Alzheimer's disease at the Veterans Administration Medical Center in Bedford. "It's a fun thing to do with your pet," Meyer said.

Joe Dzekevich of Harvard was presented the Human Hero Award. While walking through the woods last fall with his dog, he heard the cries of two other dogs. He found one dog had locked his jaw beneath the collar of the other while playing, and they were strangling each other.

One of the dogs, Wooley, was unconscious. Dzekevich cut the dogs free and performed mouth-to-mouth resuscitation and CPR on Wooley, saving his

Award was given to Tim enth graders

Eliott, an Amazon parrot credited with family of East Boston. edal he recei

My Puppy

It's funny
my puppy
knows just how I feel.

When I'm happy
he's yappy
and squirms like an eel.

When I'm grumpy
he's slumpy
and stays at my heel.

It's funny
my puppy
knows such a great deal.

by Aileen Fisher

The Goldfish

My darling little goldfish
Hasn't any toes;
He swims around without a sound
And bumps his hungry nose.

He can't get out to play with me,
Nor I get in to him,
Although I say: "Come out and play,"
And he — "Come in and swim."

by Dorothy Aldis

A discovery!
On my frog's smooth, green belly
there sits no button.

Haiku by Yayû

Make a Funny Comic Strip

by Charles M. Schulz

Humor has to come from your own personality and experiences. If you're going to draw a comic strip about a funny dog, that's all right *if* you happen to own a funny dog. If you don't, you don't know how funny they can be.

Think of jokes and funny stories, and develop characters out of them.

61

MEET Angela Johnson

"I started writing when I was nine," says Angela Johnson. "My parents bought me a diary. I wrote in it every day, mostly about my friends. I also started writing poetry around the same time. Poetry was always my first love. Most of the poetry I wrote then was about trees and flowers, and I remember that it made me very happy."

MEET Dav Pilkey

Dav Pilkey wrote and illustrated his first book when he was nineteen years old. He entered the book, *World War Won*, in a national writing contest. And he won!

JULIUS

STORY BY ANGELA JOHNSON
PICTURES BY DAV PILKEY

FRAGILE

Maya's granddaddy lived in Alabama, but wintered in Alaska.

He told Maya that was the reason he
liked ice cubes in his coffee.

On one of Granddaddy's visits from
Alaska, he brought a crate.
A surprise for Maya!
"Something that will teach you fun
and sharing." Granddaddy smiled.
"Something for my special you."

HANDLE
WITH
CARE

Maya hoped it was a horse or an older brother.

She'd always wanted one or the other.

But it was a pig.

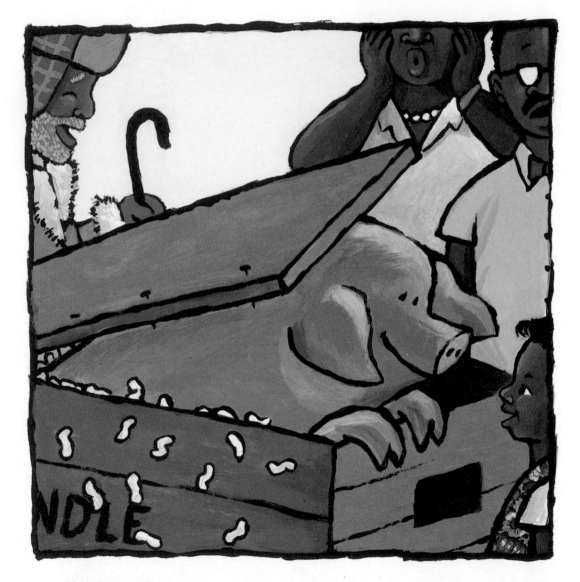

A big pig.
An Alaskan pig, who did a polar bear
imitation and climbed out of the crate.

Julius had come.

69

Maya's parents didn't think that they
would like Julius.
He showed them no fun, no sharing.

Maya loved Julius, though, so he stayed.

There never was enough food in the
house after Julius came to stay.
    He slurped coffee and ate too much
peanut butter.

He would roll himself in flour when
he wanted Maya to bake him cookies.

Julius made big messes and spread
the newspaper everywhere before
anyone could read it.

He left crumbs on the sheets and
never picked up his towels.

Julius made too much noise. He'd
stay up late watching old movies,

and he'd always play records when
everybody else wanted to read.

But Maya knew the other Julius too. . . .

The Julius who was fun to take on walks 'cause he did great dog imitations and chased cats.

The Julius who sneaked into stores
with her and tried on clothes.
Julius liked anything blue and stretchy.

They'd try on hats too.
Maya liked red felt.
Julius liked straw — it tasted better.

Trying on shoes was hard, though. . . .

Julius would swing for hours on the playground with Maya.

He'd protect her from the scary
things at night too . . . sometimes.

**Maya loved the Julius who taught
her how to dance to jazz records . . .**

and eat peanut butter from the jar, without getting any on the ceiling.

Maya didn't think all the older brothers in the world could have taught her that.

Julius loved the Maya who taught
him that even though he was a pig he
didn't have to act like he lived in a barn.

Julius didn't think all the Alaskan pigs
in the world could have taught him that.

Maya shared the things she'd learned
from Julius with her friends.
Swinging . . .

trying on hats, and dancing to jazz
records.

Julius shared the things Maya had
taught him with her parents . . . sometimes.

And that was all right, because living
with Maya and sharing everything
was even better than being a cool pig
from Alaska.

Mind Your Manners!

Julius didn't always mind his manners. With a partner, make a list of rules that will help Julius use good manners. Include the ones from the story. Think up some of your own. Then choose a way to share your ideas.

- **Use your list to make a book called *Julius's Book of Manners*.**

- **Pantomime the rules. Have the class guess what they are.**

Bunches of Babies

Largest
Pet
Litters

12 guinea pigs

23 dogs

19 cats

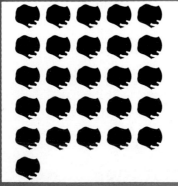

26 hamsters

14 gerbils

34 mice

93

DID YOU KNOW?

Here, Spot!

Dalmatian puppies are born white. They start to get their spots when they are about five weeks old.

Hogwash

Pigs are not really dirty animals that just eat garbage. Because pigs have thick skin, they get hot easily. They roll in mud to cool off. As for the garbage — they eat it because that's what their owners often feed them.

Happy Bird Day!

Some pets live a really long time.
One cockatoo in a London zoo
lived to be 120 years old.

Something Fishy

Goldfish are not always gold.
If they are kept in low light,
or if they live in moving water,
such as a stream, they lose
their color.

Taking Care of Biz

by Robert Price

One day my dog, Biz, stopped eating. He just lay there on the living room rug. It's weird — I can't explain it, but when Biz feels bad, I feel bad too.

I told my mom, and she said she'd leave work early so we could take Biz to the veterinarian (vet-uh-rih-NAIR-ee-uhn).

When we got there, Biz laid his sad head in Mom's lap. After a few minutes, the vet called us into his office. Dr. Moore was one nice guy right from the start. He asked us a whole bunch of questions about Biz.

The neatest thing was how he talked to Biz. I never saw Biz like anyone so quickly! He looked right up into the vet's eyes and stayed still as a statue while Dr. Moore examined him. It didn't take the doctor long to figure out that Biz had a stomach virus.

For the next five days, I had to give Biz a pill every morning and every night. And by the weekend he was his old self again — jumping all over me.

All this got me thinking. See, I always said I wanted to be a firefighter when I grow up. But now . . . I keep thinking about Dr. Moore. And now I think I want to be a vet. I even went and checked out a book at the library about veterinarians.

I found out that vets don't work just in clinics. They can work on horse farms or cattle ranches — or even at zoos or race-tracks. But there are only 27 vet colleges in the whole United States. So I have to do super well in school to be able to get into one of them.

Could I still be a firefighter on the weekends? Hmm, I don't know — I'll figure it all out later. Right now I'm going to go play Frisbee with Biz.

BE A NATURE DETECTIVE

White Birch
Bark

Gull
Feather

Tadpoles

Animal Tracks

Written and illustrated by
Arthur Dorros

BIG BOOK **PLUS**

Animal Tracks
by Arthur Dorros

Table of Contents

WATCH **ME** READ

WATCH **ME** READ

WATCH **ME** READ

WATCH **ME** READ

Finding Animal Tracks

What Can Jenna Find?

Raccoon and Lizard Take a Hike

Karen's Island

SPIDERS
PAPERBACK **PLUS**
BY GAIL GIBBONS

More Books You Can Read!

Meet Shelley Rotner and Ken Kreisler

Shelley Rotner didn't write children's books until she had a daughter of her own. She says, "My daughter always loved to look at books, and as she grew, I started to think and write about the subjects that interested her."

Ken Kreisler loves the outdoors. He was a United States Coast Guard captain for many years. He also worked as a fisherman.

Shelley Rotner and Ken Kreisler have also worked together on the books *Ocean Day, Faces,* and *Citybook*.

NATURE SPY

written by SHELLEY ROTNER and KEN KREISLER
photographs by SHELLEY ROTNER

I like to go outside — to look around and
discover things.

To take a really close look, even closer

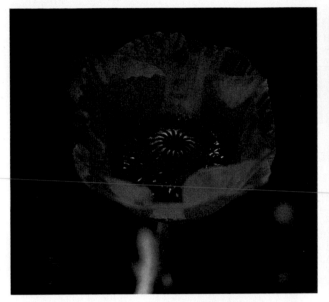 

and closer.

My mother says I'm a curious kid. She calls me a nature spy.

Sometimes I look so closely, I can see the lines on a shiny green leaf,

or one small acorn on a branch, or seeds in a pod.

I notice the feathers
of a bird,

or the golden eye of a frog.

When you look closely, things look
so different — like the bark of a tree or an
empty hornet's nest,

the seeds of a sunflower, or even a rock.

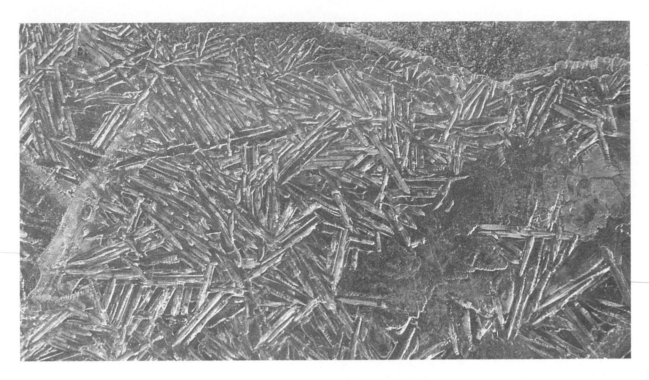

Sometimes there's a pattern, like ice
on a frozen pond,

or a spider's web, or a butterfly's wing.

Everything has its own shape, color, and size.
Look closely at a turtle's shell,

or a dog's fur,

or even raspberries, or kernels of corn.

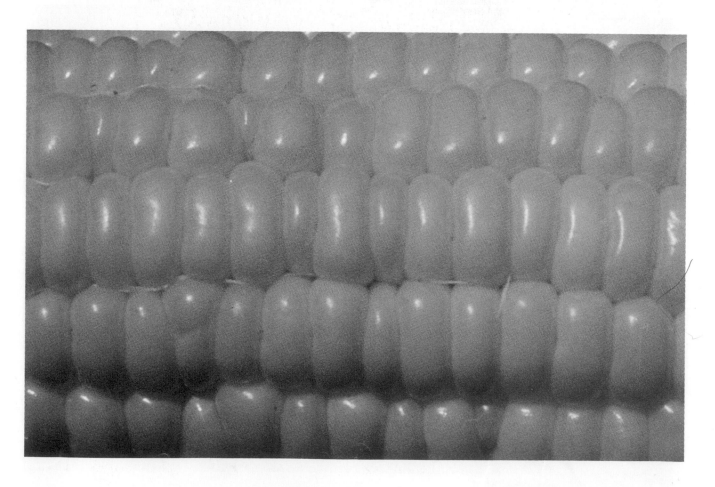

No matter where you look, up, down or all around,

there's always something to see when you're a nature spy!

Take a Closer Look

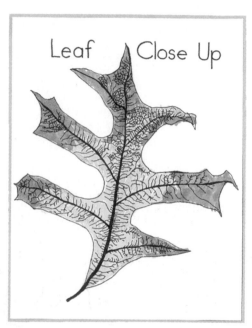

Be a nature detective like the girl in the story. Find an object, such as a leaf, a flower, or bark from a tree. Look at it up close. Draw a picture of what you see. Then draw another picture, looking at the object from far away. What did you see up close that you didn't see from far away?

Hiding Place

Down among the cobwebs, at the roots of grass

Green and creepy quiet, dewy beads of glass

Little spiders spinning, beetles bumbling through

Ants in hurry-scurries, bustling on my shoe

Tiny flowers bending when the bees weigh them down

And bouncing up fluttering the butterflies around

Down among the cobwebs and the grasshopper spittle

I can hide and peek around and be glad I am little.

by Nancy Dingman Watson

To Catch a THIEF

Dear Ranger Rick,

We had a funny thing happen in our neighborhood. Only it wasn't funny when it was happening.

I woke up one morning and went outside to sit in our yard. Soon my friend Brook woke up and came out too. (He was living with us.) When Brook got to the front porch he yelled, "Where are my shoes?" Then I realized that my shoes — my Air Jordans — were missing too! We had left them out on the porch the night before.

My Air Jordans were my favorite shoes. I was really upset. Could it be someone playing a joke, or was there a real thief out there?

That night at dinner, Brook, Mom, Dad, and I talked about the missing shoes. I thought that maybe we could make a push-button switch that would turn on when a shoe was lifted off it. Then we could catch the shoe bandit if he or she came back. My dad thought that was a great idea.

So the next day we bought a push-button switch. Once we'd figured out how to rig it up, we hooked the switch up to a spare car horn. We tried it a few times, and it worked great. Now all we had to do was wait until nighttime, and maybe we'd catch the thief.

Here's a photo of me with just some of the shoes.

Ranger Rick Magazine
8925 Leesburg Pike
Vienna, VA 22184

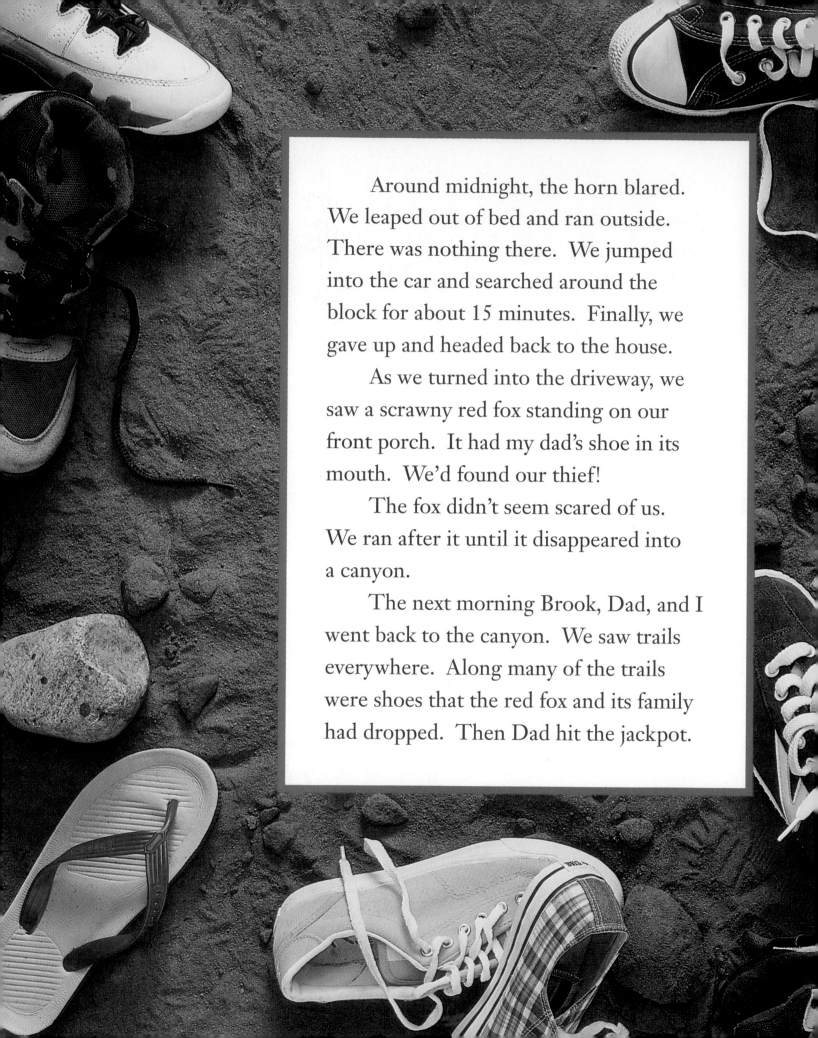

Around midnight, the horn blared. We leaped out of bed and ran outside. There was nothing there. We jumped into the car and searched around the block for about 15 minutes. Finally, we gave up and headed back to the house.

As we turned into the driveway, we saw a scrawny red fox standing on our front porch. It had my dad's shoe in its mouth. We'd found our thief!

The fox didn't seem scared of us. We ran after it until it disappeared into a canyon.

The next morning Brook, Dad, and I went back to the canyon. We saw trails everywhere. Along many of the trails were shoes that the red fox and its family had dropped. Then Dad hit the jackpot.

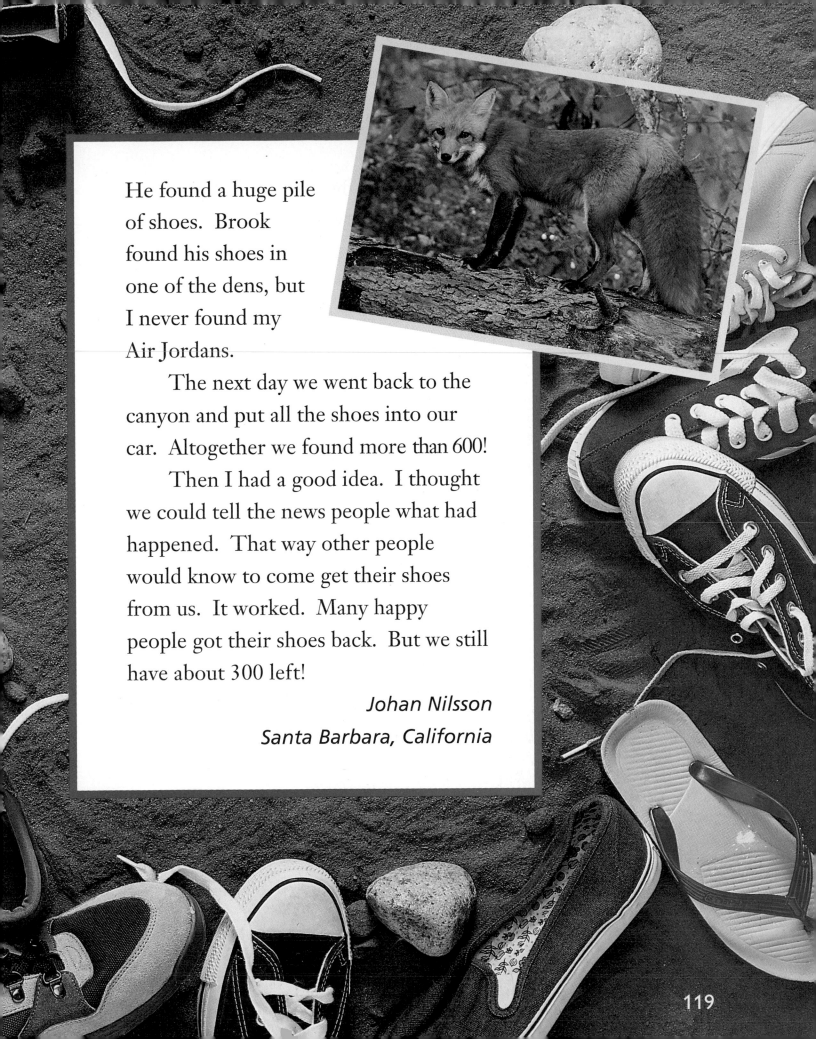

He found a huge pile of shoes. Brook found his shoes in one of the dens, but I never found my Air Jordans.

The next day we went back to the canyon and put all the shoes into our car. Altogether we found more than 600!

Then I had a good idea. I thought we could tell the news people what had happened. That way other people would know to come get their shoes from us. It worked. Many happy people got their shoes back. But we still have about 300 left!

Johan Nilsson
Santa Barbara, California

MY NATURE JOURNAL

by Carolyn Duckworth

You can keep a nature journal no matter where you are. Even if you live in a city, you can write about what you see out your window or in a city park.

WHAT YOU NEED

• **Notebook** Before you buy one, think about how you'll carry it. Will it need to fit in your pocket, a belt pack, or a back pack? Also, do you want a notebook with paper bound in or a binder you can add pages to?

• **Paper** Do you want blank paper or lined paper? It may be easier to write on lined paper, but drawings may look nicer – and be more fun – on blank paper.

• **Something to write and draw with** You can sketch with the same pen or pencil you write with and then fill in colors at home. Just be sure to write down the colors of the plant or animal that you've sketched.

• **Go outdoors** – anywhere. Sit on your front porch, walk around the edge of a parking lot, go for a hike – just get outside! Take your notebook with you.

• **Ask questions.** What's different about today? What sounds do you hear? What do you smell? Can you see any animals? What are they doing? With words or drawings, answer these questions in your journal.

• **Show and tell.** When you draw an animal or plant, pay attention to all the details. Does it have stripes or dots on its back or head? How many petals are on the flower, and how are they arranged? Is it smaller than your little finger? Colors are important too. Finally, write down where you saw the plant or animal and exactly what it was doing.

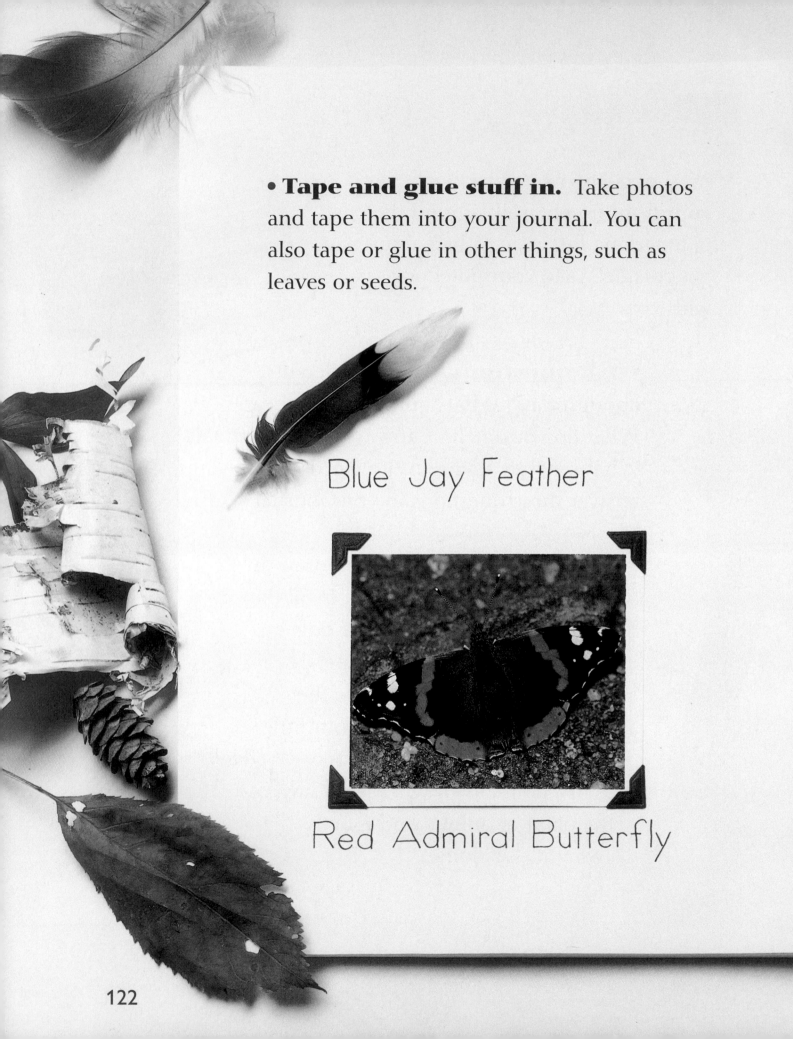

• **Tape and glue stuff in.** Take photos and tape them into your journal. You can also tape or glue in other things, such as leaves or seeds.

Blue Jay Feather

Red Admiral Butterfly

• **Find that name.** At home or in the library, you may want to use a *field guide* to look up the plants and animals you've seen. If you've described the plant or animal carefully, you can often find it in a field guide – or find something that's close.

You can have a lot of fun keeping a nature journal. Hope you try it!

Peterson
First Guides®
WILD-
FLOWERS

A simplified field guide
to the common wildflowers
...theastern and
...orth America

Meet
Kathleen Weidner Zoehfeld

Kathleen Weidner Zoehfeld has always loved the outdoors. She grew up on a farm in the mountains, where she hiked in the woods with her father and granddad. She no longer lives in the mountains, but she still enjoys nature-watching with her family at the beach not far from her home in Connecticut.

The author with her son, Geoffrey

Helen Davie at work in her studio. Can you find the shells?

Meet
Helen K. Davie

When Helen Davie was small, her family would often go to the beach. She spent a lot of time on the shore collecting shells, since she couldn't swim that well. Ms. Davie used shells as models for her illustrations. She even kept a live snail in a jar on her desk!

What Lives in a Shell?

Shell?

STAGE 1

by Kathleen Weidner Zoehfeld • illustrated by Helen K. Davie

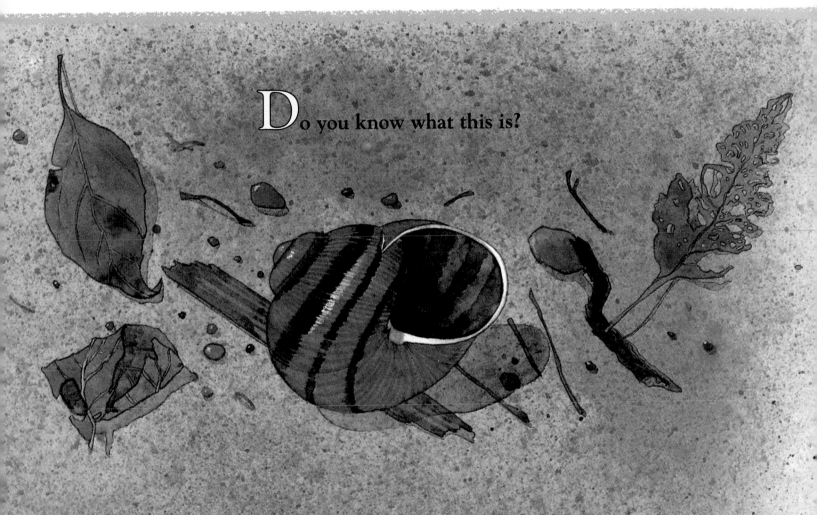

Do you know what this is?

It is as hard as a stone. But it is not a stone.

It is smooth, like glass. But it is not glass.

It is hollow inside, like a cup. But it is not a cup.

It is a shell. An animal made it. The shell was the animal's home.

You live in a house or in an apartment building.
That is your home. Your home keeps you safe and warm.

Lots of animals have homes.
Birds build nests.

Ants make tunnels underground.

A bear likes to live in a cave.

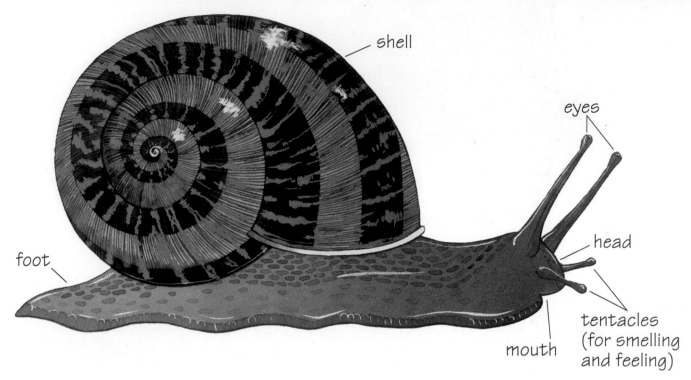

shell

eyes

head

tentacles
(for smelling
and feeling)

foot

mouth

Here is the animal that lives in this kind of shell.
It is a land snail.

A land snail is born with a tiny shell. As long as
the snail lives, it keeps on growing.

As the snail grows, its shell grows with it. The
shell keeps the snail safe.

You can go in and out of your home. You can run to the playground. You can wait outside for the bus.

A snail never leaves its home. It takes its home with it wherever it goes.

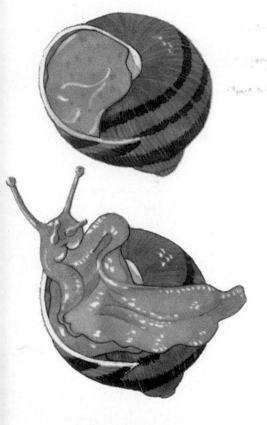

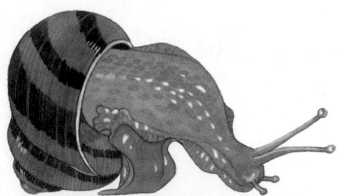

The snail pokes its soft
head and its one big foot
out of the opening in its
shell. It uses its foot to inch
along. A snail is slow.

Birds like to eat snails. When a bird or other enemy comes around, a snail cannot run away. It pulls its head and foot inside its shell and closes the door. The snail is safe.

Other kinds of animals live in shells, too. Shells come in many shapes, colors, and sizes.

Turtles live in shells. A turtle's shell can be bumpy or smooth. Most are rounded on top and flat on the belly.

Baby turtles have little shells. As the babies grow bigger, their shells grow bigger.

A turtle has four legs. It pokes its legs, head, and tail through the openings in its shell. Even though it has four legs, a turtle is slow.

Have you ever had a turtle race?

If a frog and a turtle were in a race, who do you think would win?

What about a cat and a turtle?

If a turtle sees a cat, it may be frightened. It may think the cat wants to eat it.

A turtle cannot run as fast as a cat. The turtle pulls its head and legs and tail into its shell. The cat pats the turtle with its paw. The turtle won't come out. It is safe in its shell home.

When you go to the seashore, you can find many different kinds of shells.

You may see a crab walking on the sand. A crab has ten legs. On its front legs are two claws. A hard shell covers its claws and the rest of its body.

A crab's shell fits it like a suit of armor. The armor helps keep the crab safe from enemies.

But just as you outgrow your favorite shirt, a crab outgrows its shell. When it gets too tight, the crab pulls itself out. Underneath is a new shell.

You may find snails buried in the sand. Some of them do not look much like the land snails.

Whelks and conchs are types of snails that are found only by the sea. Here are some different kinds of sea-snail shells.

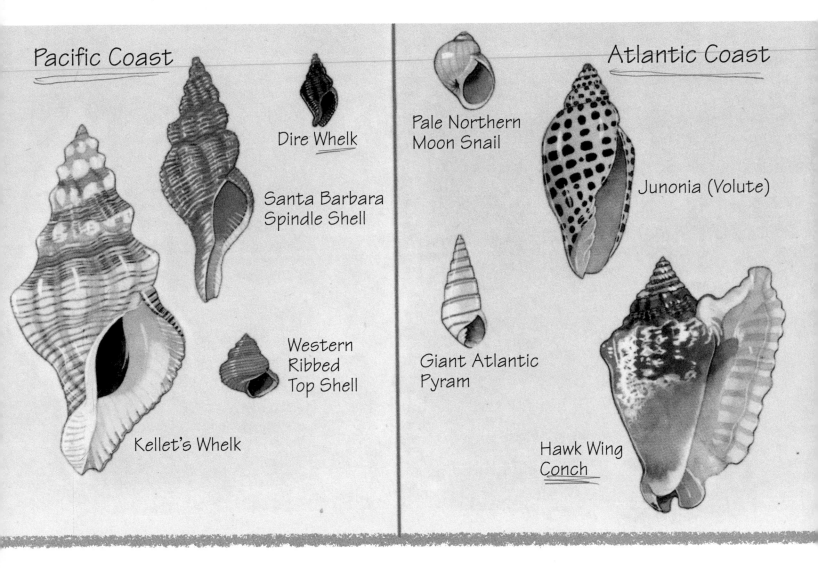

Pacific Coast

Dire Whelk

Santa Barbara Spindle Shell

Western Ribbed Top Shell

Kellet's Whelk

Pale Northern Moon Snail

Atlantic Coast

Junonia (Volute)

Giant Atlantic Pyram

Hawk Wing Conch

Have you ever seen a snail shell walking along on crab legs?

A hermit crab has hard claws in front, but the back end of its body has a soft shell. Its shell is too soft to keep it safe from enemies.

A hermit crab lives in an empty snail shell.

After a while the hermit crab grows too big for his shell. So he looks for a bigger one. Some are too big. Some are too small. Finally he finds one he likes. He throws away the old shell and crawls into the new one.

Now the new shell is his home. The snail shell helps keep him safe.

 clam shell
outside

oyster shell
outside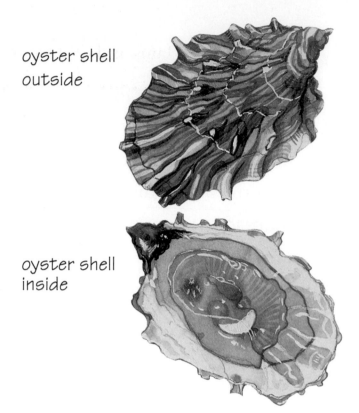

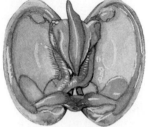 clam shell
inside

clam shell
hinge

oyster shell
inside

You can look for clam and oyster shells at the
beach, too. Clams and oysters are animals.
They have no legs. They do not have heads or
tails. Their bodies are soft. But they are animals.

Clams and oysters grow two hard shells. The top shell and bottom shell look almost alike. The two shells are connected by a hinge. Scallops also have two shells. Here are some different kinds of scallop shells.

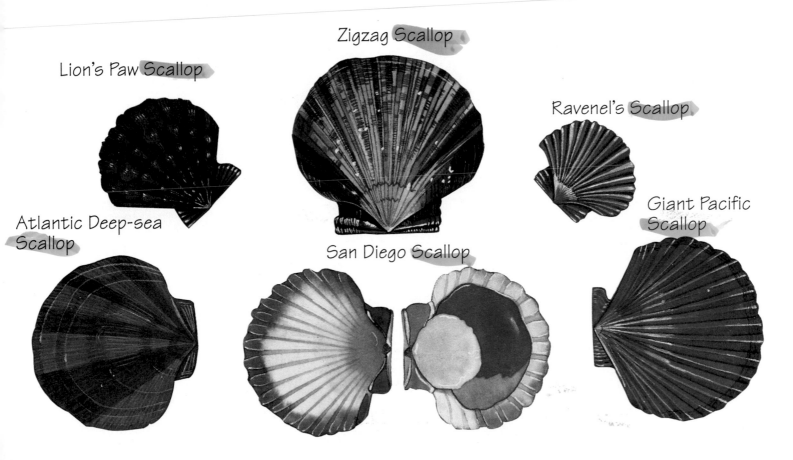

Zigzag Scallop

Lion's Paw Scallop

Ravenel's Scallop

Atlantic Deep-sea Scallop

San Diego Scallop

Giant Pacific Scallop

Most clams and oysters hardly move at all. They open up their shells to take in food and water. They close their shells tightly when enemies are around.

Some scallops can swim. A scallop does not swim like a fish, though. First it opens its two shells. Then it snaps them together quickly. This gets the scallop where it wants to go.

When you find a shell, carefully look inside.

It will probably be empty. If a shell is empty, it may mean the animal has died. Or, it has outgrown the shell and left it behind.

If the animal is at home, you can watch it for a while. See if you can tell how it eats. How does it move? What does it do when it feels frightened?

When you go, leave the animal where you found it. Animals are happiest in their natural surroundings. If a shell is empty, you can take it home with you.

If you are looking at shells in a state or national park, be sure to ask a ranger or game warden before you take any shells from the park.

Try to find as many different kinds of shells as you can. Whether the shells you find are big or small, plain or fancy — remember, a shell is someone's home.

Shell Secrets

It has legs and moves sideways.

Make shell riddles. First, fold a piece of paper in half. Then pick one of the shell animals from the story. Draw a picture of the animal on the inside of the folded paper. Write a riddle on the outside. See if a partner can answer your riddle.

Build a Bug Home!

What things make a home
snug for a bug?
Find out here.

— You Need —

Clear jar

Handful of soil

Rock

Leaf

Wet cotton ball

Rubber band

Piece of old stocking

Bug

1. First, put the soil in the jar. Add the rock, leaf, and wet cotton ball. How will your bug use these things?

2. Second, place your bug in the jar.

3. Next, ask a grownup to help you find out what your bug eats. Add its food to the jar.

4. Then put the stocking over the jar's opening. Use the rubber band to hold it in place.

5. Finally, watch your bug for a few days. Record what it does. Then put your bug back where you found it.

My Bug

Think about it
What things does your bug need to live? What things do you need to live?

How to Make a Terrarium

Instructions by Charles Ervin Helms

How do you make a terrarium? Charles wrote these instructions that tell you how he did it, step by step.

How to Make a Terrarium

This is how I made my terrarium. First, I got a jar. Then I put rocks in the bottom of the jar. Next, I went outside for sand. I put a cup of sand on top of the rocks. I poured in about one-half cup of pine chips. Next, I put a cupful of dirt in the jar. Then I planted plants and watered them. I placed my decorations, which were a gold rock and a pecan. Finally, I put on the lid. My terrarium looked wonderful!

Charles Ervin Helms
Highland Elementary School
Charlotte, North Carolina

Charles made a terrarium in second grade.
Then he wrote these instructions because he
really liked the way the terrarium turned out.
Charles also likes to swim and play ball. He
would like to be a teacher when he grows up.

155

Purple Finches

Project FeederWatch

by Cynthia Berger

Flocks of finches, colorful cardinals, and all kinds of other birds are flying to feeders at schools and in backyards. While the birds collect a meal, kids are collecting important information for scientists.

Scientists want to keep track of birds in North America. So the kids send them the information they collect. The kids are part of a program called Project FeederWatch — together with 7000 other kids and adults in the United States and Canada. The youngest FeederWatcher is five. The oldest? 91!

Sometimes we use a bird book called a *field guide* to help us find the name of a bird.

Our classroom is great for bird watching. With binoculars, we can see what's happening at the feeder, and we don't bother the birds while we watch them.

"We have a list of bird names, and we mark down which birds we see," says Sabrina Budny from Manorhaven School in Port Washington, New York.

FeederWatchers have to really know the birds at their feeders. They also have to be able to follow the rules for counting them.

Evening Grosbeaks

Cardinal

"Learning the birds' names was pretty easy," explains James Gibbons. "At first our class knew only a few. Now we can identify 23 different kinds!"

Watching Birds at School

Some kids watch feeders at home with their parents. But the kids in this story did a special FeederWatch project at several schools in New York. One thing they tried to find out was what kinds of seeds birds like best.

Birds were a part of almost every subject at our school. We weighed the bird seed as part of our math lessons. Our hungry birds ate almost 200 pounds (90 kg) of seeds last winter!

159

All of us kids in Project FeederWatch agreed: Working on the project was really more *fun* than work. Here we are filling a feeder with safflower seeds.

Goldfinches

Birds We Ha

1.
2.
3.
4.
5.
6.
7.
8.
9.
10.

The kids used two matching feeders. One was filled with sunflower seeds and the other with safflower seeds. Every day during five-minute count periods, the kids wrote down how many birds visited each feeder. They discovered that the birds ate a lot more sunflower seeds than safflower seeds.

This winter, the school kids are testing other kinds of seeds.

We used computers to trade bird information with kids at other schools. One class only saw crows. But we had exciting news — a sharp-shinned hawk ate at our feeder.

Helping the Scientists

Why do scientists want the FeederWatchers to count how many birds — and what kinds — come to the feeders? One reason is that scientists want to know *where* the birds are. For example, cardinals

Pine Grosbeak

used to live only in the southern and central parts of the United States. Now these birds are moving northward. By counting birds at feeders, FeederWatchers keep track of how different birds are spreading across North America.

Scientists also want to know if any kinds of birds are getting rare. Most feeder birds aren't in danger of becoming *extinct* (dying out). But if the FeederWatch scientists learn that some birds are getting rare, they may be able to do something quickly to help them.

Meet Burton Albert

When Burton Albert was a boy, he raised chickens and rabbits, fished for trout, and delivered newspapers. One of his first jobs as an adult was teaching school. One of his sixth grade students later became an author of children's books — just like he did!

Meet Brian Pinkney

Brian Pinkney says, "I make pictures for the child in me. My work is actually my way of playing." *Where Does the Trail Lead?* reminds him of his own childhood summers on Cape Cod in Massachusetts.

Brian Pinkney, Age 9

Where Does the Trail Lead?

By Burton Albert
Illustrated by Brian Pinkney

On Summertime Island,
where does the trail lead?
Over hills and hollows
of buttercups and snapdragons . . .

. . . to a lighthouse at the edge of the sea.

Where does the trail lead?
Past tree limbs bent by the wind,
and tide-pools of periwinkles . . .

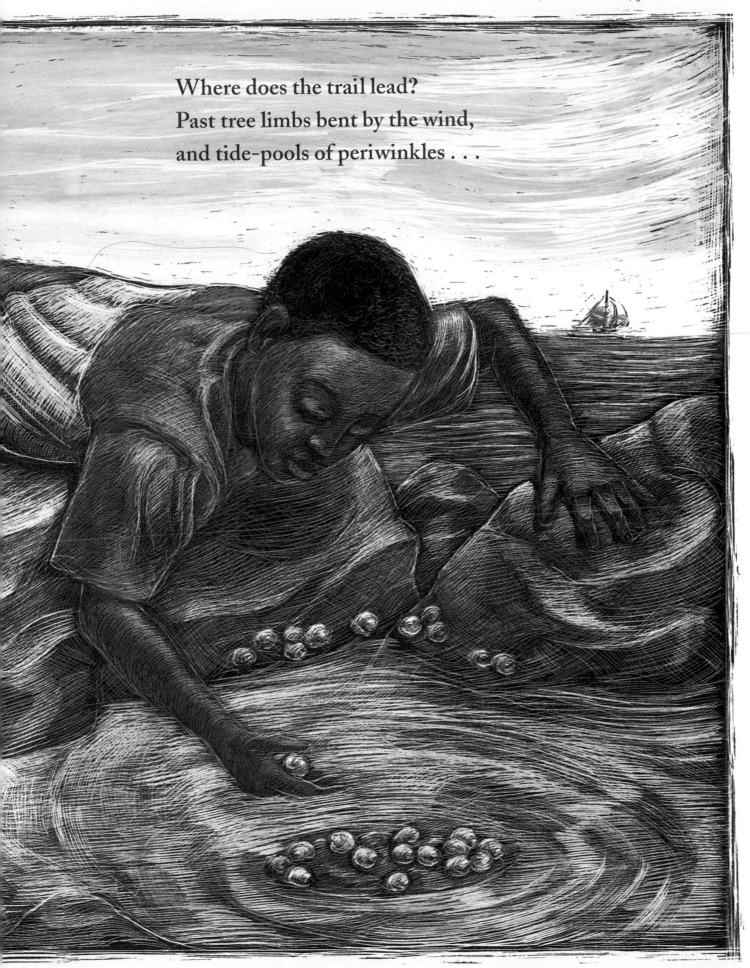

. . . to gulls in flight at the edge of the sea.

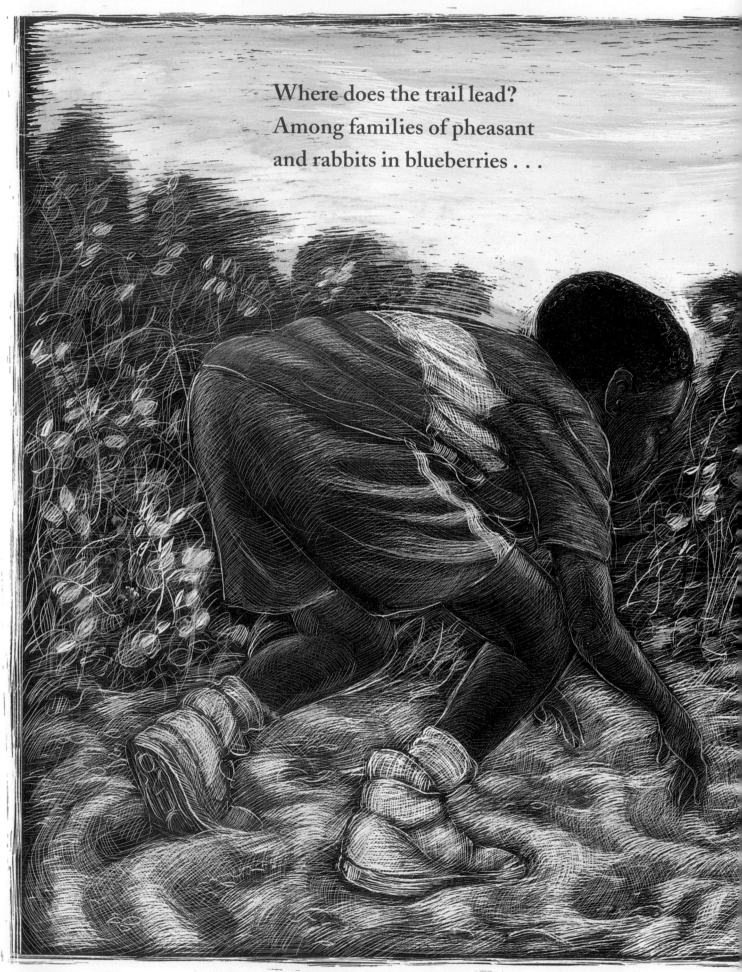

Where does the trail lead?
Among families of pheasant
and rabbits in blueberries . . .

172

173

. . . to a crest of dunes
at the edge of the sea.

On Summertime Island
where does the trail lead?
Beside old tracks, grown over with grass,
where a rickety train once ran . . .

. . . to a ghost town of shanties at the edge of the sea.

Where does the trail lead?
Over the crunch of pine needles — dried and brown.
Beneath the V's and honks of geese . . .

. . . to a boat's bow of cattails at the edge of the sea.

183

Where does the trail lead?
Down a zig-zag of ruts from trucks in the sand.
Along railings of fence on a rocky rim . . .

. . . to the roar of surfers' waves
at the edge of the sea.

186

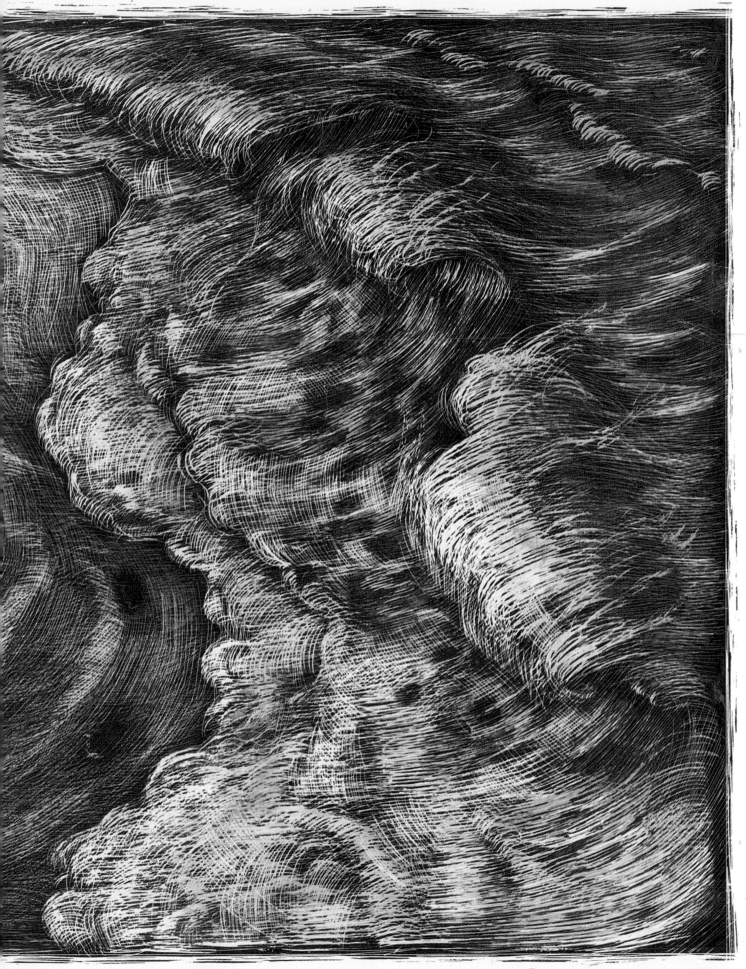

On Summertime Island,
where does the trail lead?
Back to the crackle of campfires
and the smell of fresh-caught fish . . .

. . . to the shimmerings
and shadows of a sinking sun

in the twilight at the edge of the sea.

Adventures on Summertime Island

Think about the things you would see if you took a trip to Summertime Island. Choose a way to share your ideas.

- Make a post card to send to a friend. On the back, tell your friend about the island.

- Make a mural of Summertime Island. Draw the trail and some of the things along the trail. Work with a group or a partner.

Go on a Leaf Hunt!

Who can find the biggest leaf? The reddest one? The one most like a dinosaur? Then match your leaves with ours.

box elder

birch

scarlet oak

ginkgo

downy arrowwood

yellow oak

white oak

smooth sumac

To cock-a-doodle do the rooster, use long, feathery leaves to make its tail and neck and small leaves for its claws.

shagbark hickory

willow

bittersweet

beach pine

white pine

dogwood

blueberry

Making an animal like a mouse? Be sure to get a few leaves with long stems for its tail. And don't forget little leaves for its eyes and nose.

sassafras

Frog or Toad:
How to Tell

by Elizabeth A. Lacey

FROGS AND TOADS have the same overall shape and often seem much alike in color and habits. Both of these amphibians, for instance, usually lay their eggs in or near water.

Generally speaking, if you find it in a pond, it's the common frog, and if you find it in the woods, it's the common toad. But there are other clues as well.

The Common Frog	The Common Toad
Smooth, soft skin	Thick, bumpy skin
Long ridges down each side of back	Short ridges on top of head, largish bumps behind eyes
Largish round "ears" under eyes on each side	Very small round "ears" below eyes
Slender body, long legs, speedy swimmer	Plump body, shorter legs, slower moving
Lives in or very near water	Lives on land, in woods
Small teeth in upper jaw only	No teeth
Clumps of eggs laid in water	Strands of eggs laid in water
Male has eardrums larger than eyes.	Male usually has dark toes and throat.

Good
Friends

My First American Friend
by Sarunna Jin
illustrated by Shirley V. Beckes

200

Table of Contents

Next Door Friends

The Great Outdoors

Sonny's Best Friend

Harry and Friends in the Old West

WATCH **ME** READ

PAPERBACK **PLUS**

More Books You Can Read!

Meet Patricia Reilly Giff

Patricia Reilly Giff likes to write about kids. She says, "I think of a zippy kid. I lie in the middle of the living room rug, I shut my eyes, and I try to think about somebody who is funny, and quick, and lively."

Many of the characters in Patricia Reilly Giff's stories are like people she knows in real life. Ronald Morgan is a lot like one of the students she used to teach in school.

Meet Susanna Natti

Then . . .

Susanna Natti knew she was going to be an illustrator by the time she was eight. She and her favorite cousin had drawing contests. She doesn't remember that they ever compared their pictures, but they had a lot of fun drawing!

Susanna, Lydia, Alan, and Kate

And Now

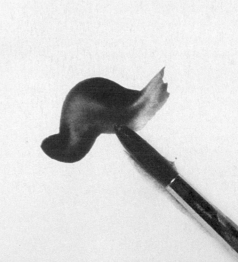

Susanna Natti drew this picture of her family.

Watch Out, Ronald Morgan!

by Patricia Reilly Giff

illustrated by Susanna Natti

It all started when the bell rang. I raced
across the school yard and slid over a patch
of ice.

"Watch out!" Rosemary yelled. But it was
too late. I bumped into her and she landed in a
snow pile.

After I hung up my jacket, I fed the
goldfish. I fed Frank, the gerbil, too.

"Oh, no," Rosemary said. "You fed the
gerbil food to Goldie."

"Oh," I said. "The boxes look the same."

Billy shook his head. "Can't you read the
letters? F is for fish. G is for gerbil."

"Don't worry," said Michael, my best friend.
He poured more water into the fish tank.

At recess Miss Tyler wouldn't let us go outside. "You'll get snow in your sneakers," she said. So we played kickball in the gym. The ball bounced off my head.

Marc said, "I'm glad you're not on my team."

And Rosemary said, "Can't you even see the ball?"

Then it was time for book reports. "Who'd like to be first?" Miss Tyler asked. I ducked behind my desk.

"Ronald Morgan," said Miss Tyler.

"My book is *Lennie Lion*," I said.

I held up my report and blinked to see the
words. "This book is about a lion named
Lennie. He's ferocious and good."

"Great," said Jan.

"Grr," said Michael.

"Lovely," said Miss Tyler.

After lunch we looked out the window.
Everything was white. "It's time for a winter
classroom," said Miss Tyler.

I bent over my desk and drew a snowflake.
Then I cut it out.

Tom said, "Ronald Morgan, that's a wiggly
snowflake. Why don't you cut on the lines?"

And Rosemary said, "I think your snowflake
is melting."

When it was time to go home, Miss Tyler gave me a note for my mother and father. "Maybe you need glasses," she said.

At lunch the next day, Marc asked, "When do you get your glasses?"

I took a bite of my peanut butter sandwich. "I go to the doctor today."

And Michael asked, "Can I go with you?"

In the shopping mall we passed my father's
tie store. I waved to him and he waved back.

In Doctor Sims's window was a huge pair of
eyeglasses. Michael and I made believe they
belonged to a monster.

"Look at these Es," said Doctor Sims. "Which way do they point?"

I squinted my eyes and pointed. The Es looked smaller and smaller.

Then Doctor Sims said, "It's hard for you to see them."

And my mother said, "You'll look great in glasses."

"Yes," said the doctor. "Glasses will help. They'll make everything look sharp and clear."

Next we went to the counter. I tried on a pair of red frames. They slid down over my nose.

I tried round ones and square ones. Then I put on blue frames and looked in the mirror.

"Good," said my mother.

"Good," said Michael.

And Doctor Sims said, "The lenses will be ready in an hour."

We went to the tie store. "My glasses are great," I told my father.

He smiled. "Now everything will look the way it should," he said.

Then my glasses were ready. "Just wait till tomorrow," I said. "I'll be the best ballplayer, the best reader, the best speller, the best everything."

"Wow," said Michael.

"Nice," said my mother.

"Yes," I told them. "I'll be the superkid of the school."

Before school, I threw some snowballs.
"You missed!" Jimmy yelled, and threw one at
me. It landed right on my nose.

Rosemary laughed. "Your glasses need
windshield wipers," she said.

But Michael looked worried. "How come
your glasses don't work?"

In the classroom, I hung up my jacket and put my hat on the shelf.

"Where is our fish monitor?" asked Miss Tyler.

I ran to give Goldie some food. This time I looked at the box. The letters looked big and sharp. "G is for Goldie," I said. "F is for Frank."

"Oh, no," said Billy. "F is for fish. G is for gerbil."

And Michael frowned. "I don't think your glasses help."

I tiptoed into the closet and put the glasses
inside my hat.

Alice looked at me. "Where are your blue
glasses?" she whispered.

I shook my head. "I have terrible glasses.
I'll never be the superkid of the class."

When it was time to go home, Miss Tyler gave me another note. My mother helped me with some of the words.

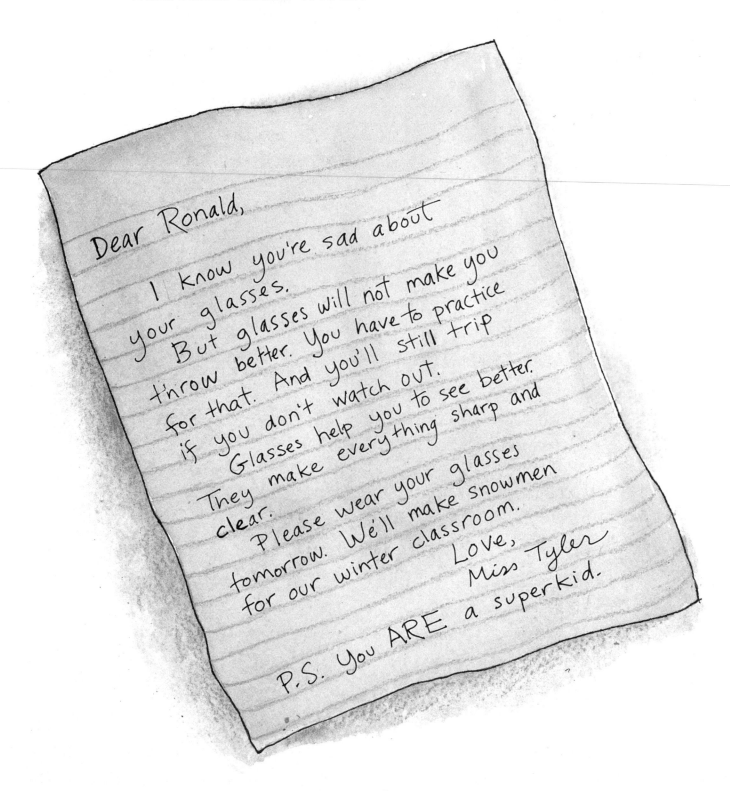

Dear Ronald,

I know you're sad about your glasses. But glasses will not make you throw better. You have to practice for that. And you'll still trip if you don't watch out. Glasses help you to see better. They make everything sharp and clear.

Please wear your glasses tomorrow. We'll make snowmen for our winter classroom.

Love,
Miss Tyler

P.S. You ARE a superkid.

In school I drew a snowman and picked up the scissors to cut. "Hey," I said, "Miss Tyler's right. The lines are sharp and clear."

"Good snowman," said Rosemary.

And Miss Tyler said, "Just what we need for our winter classroom."

I picked up my blue crayon and drew a few more lines. "Now he's a super snowman," I said. We all cheered.

Superkids!

Best Sharer

Ronald Morgan learned that everybody is a superkid in some way. Choose a partner. Think about the ways your partner is special and make a list. Pick one special thing and make a superkid award. Then give a talk to the class. Tell why your partner is a superkid.

Dear Ricardo

A Letter by Jorge Hernandez

Jorge has lots of fun at school. He wrote his friend Ricardo a letter to tell him all about it.

October 27, 1994

Dear Ricardo,

I play on the computer in my classroom. The computers have games. My favorite game is a maze game. I love it! You have to move your animal through the maze. When you get to a wall, you have to do math problems to get through. When you get to the castle, the door opens. You go inside and a horse and a bear come out for your prize.

I also play soccer at school. I am on a team. Yesterday we won. I was about to make a goal, but the goalie blocked it. Tony was about to score. Then Dereck hit the ball with his head, and he made the goal. Our team won!

Your friend,
Jorge

Jorge Hernandez
Pine Grove Elementary School
Hood River, Oregon

Jorge wrote this letter when he was in the second grade. He says, "My favorite thing to do is play soccer. When I grow up I want to be a good soccer player like my dad."

Jorge also likes to go to rodeos. He even knows how to ride a horse!

Pen Pals

by Beverly M. Lewis

Janie writes to her pen pal, Stephanie, in China.

"Getting letters is great," says 10-year-old Jonathan, as he licks two stamps and puts them on two different envelopes. "But writing them is fun, too." Jonathan has two pen pals — one in Massachusetts and one in New York. He thinks pen pals are a neat way to make friends.

Jonathan's twin sister, Janie, agrees. Her pen pal, Stephanie, lives in the People's Republic of China. Stephanie's parents are American English teachers there.

The girls write to each other about hobbies, friends, and favorite books. "Stephanie and I are best pen friends. I mark a giant X on my calendar when her letter comes. Then I write back quick, since it takes at least a week to get my letter to China."

Stephanie (on the left) is Janie's American pen pal in China. Here she clowns with her sister and dog.

226

Eric met his pen pal, Donny, an American soldier who was in the Gulf War.

Eric and his classmates wrote to Donny, an American soldier in the 1991 Persian Gulf War. After the war was over, Donny showed up in uniform at Eric's school as a surprise. Getting to meet his pen pal was terrific; but for Eric, the best thing about having a pen pal is "getting lots of mail."

Amy wishes her pen pal lived closer. Narisar (pronounced Na-REE-ser) lives in Nampaad Town, Thailand. "Narisar's envelopes have pretty stamps and are fun to save," says Amy. "But the best thing about having a pen friend in another country is learning about how different and alike we are."

Here's a photo of Narisar, Amy's pen pal in Thailand.

Friendship
IN ART

Mary and Martha by William Edmondson, 1930s

Snap the Whip by Winslow Homer, 1872

Street Scene by Allan Crite, 1934

Meet Dolores Johnson

Dolores Johnson

The author with her best friend, Marie, her brother, and her sister

Dolores Johnson signing her books

Do you remember the first day you started school, were left with a baby-sitter, or acted in a school play? Dolores Johnson does. She knows that these things are important to children, which is why she writes about them.

What Kind of Baby-sitter Is This?

written and illustrated by Dolores Johnson

Kevin's mother was getting all dressed up to go out. And then the doorbell rang.

"Not another baby-sitter!" cried Kevin.
"You said you'd take me with you next time!

If you leave me tonight I . . . I . . . I . . .
I'm not going to be your friend!"

"Kevin," said his mother. "This is Mrs.
Lovey Pritchard. She'll take care of you while
I'm away at school."

"Take a look at that face, that sweet little face," said the baby-sitter. "You can call me Aunt Lovey, sugar dumpling."

"Mom, take me with you!" yelled Kevin.

"So you're the little boy who doesn't like baby-sitters," said Aunt Lovey. "Well, we're going to have such fun together."

"Mom, don't leave me with her,
puullleeeease!" yelled Kevin.

"Don't you worry about us, little mother,"
said the baby-sitter. "Kevin and I will be
just fine."

"Well, I'm leaving, too!" said Kevin as he stormed through the kitchen out to the back porch. "That old lady will never miss me. She'll be busy doing what baby-sitters do — painting her toenails, talking on the telephone, and eating the good stuff in the refrigerator. Hey, she'd better not eat that last piece of cake!"

Kevin sneaked back into the kitchen. "Isn't she even gonna come after me? Is that lady so dumb she doesn't even know I'm gone?"

From his hiding place, Kevin heard the click
of a switch and then the roar of the television.
"So that's what she's doing. She's watching soap
operas. And my mom is paying her a zillion
dollars to watch *me*."

Aunt Lovey started yelling, jumping up and down, and clapping. "She's watching my baseball game! My *mom* wouldn't even watch it. What kind of baby-sitter is this? She's supposed to be yelling at *me*."

The baby-sitter started pulling things from her handbag. She put a baseball cap on her head. She laid some baseball cards on the couch, and she waved a pennant in the air.

"I wish she would put that pennant down,"
said Kevin. "I can hardly see."

"And it's a Badger pennant," continued
Kevin. "That proves it. She doesn't know
anything about baseball. Everybody knows that
the Badgers can't win."

When the ball game ended, and the Badgers
had won, Aunt Lovey turned off the television
set. She was so busy pulling things out of her
purse, it seems she never even noticed Kevin.

"Oh, no," said Kevin. "Here it comes
now . . . her telephone numbers . . . her
nail polish . . . those kissy-kissy books that
baby-sitters read."

But Aunt Lovey pulled out a book about
baseball, opened it, and began to read softly.

"I wish she would speak up," said Kevin.
"I can hardly hear."

So Kevin crawled closer and Aunt Lovey read louder, and they read, and played games, and told jokes, and laughed so much that they didn't even notice when Kevin's mother came home.

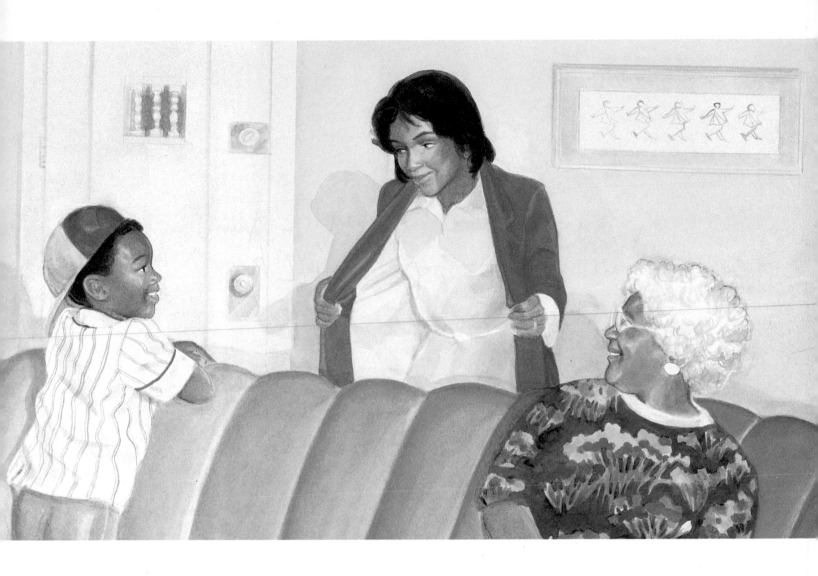

"Are you still angry with me, sweetheart?"
Kevin's mother asked when she came in. "I
really hated to leave you. But, of course, there'll
be other times when I'll have to go out."

"Well, that's all right, Mom, 'cause I've got a
great idea," said Kevin. "Can Aunt Lovey move
in with us? We can make her a bed on the
couch, or she can share your bedroom with you.
This can be her home, too."

"But, Kevin," said his mother, "Aunt Lovey
has her own home. Baby-sitters don't stay over."

"Mom, you don't understand. Aunt Lovey's
no baby-sitter — she's my friend!"

Best Baby-sitter

Kevin decided that Aunt Lovey was a great baby-sitter after all. She brought some things with her that Kevin enjoyed. What should a baby-sitter bring for you to enjoy? Work with a group or a partner. Choose a way to share your ideas.

- Make a baby-sitter's kit.
- Make a list of things that a baby-sitter should bring to your house. Read your list to the class.

Baby-sitter's Kit

247

SECRET WRITING

by Eugene Baker

To "encode" means to "put a message into code." The message is then a secret. You can send a secret message to a friend. Try this one . . .

SECRET MEETING AT LIBRARY

First, print the alphabet at the top of a sheet of paper. Then, under the "A," print a "B." Under the "B," print a "C." Do this for the entire alphabet. Under the "Z," print an "A." Your two alphabets will look like this.

A B C D E F G H I J K L M N O P Q R S T U V W X Y Z

B C D E F G H I J K L M N O P Q R S T U V W X Y Z A

SECRET WRITING

Now, print your message below the two alphabets. The first letter in your message is "S." Look at the letter below "S." It is "T." Write "T" down as the first letter in the secret code. Do this for each letter in the message. The first word becomes . . .

TFDSFU

Encode the other words. You should have . . .

TFDSFU NFFUJOH BU MJCSBSZ

Did you get it right? Now, give the message to your friend.

Numbers for Letters

A	B	C	D
1	2	3	4

E	F	G	H
5	6	7	8

I	J	K	L
9	10	11	12

M	N	O	P
13	14	15	16

Q	R	S	T
17	18	19	20

U	V	W	X
21	22	23	24

Y	Z
25	26

Some secret writing uses only numbers. The numbers take the place of letters in the alphabet. Here is a simple way to use code numbers. Encode this message . . .

YOU ARE BEING WATCHED

"YOU" becomes 25 – 15 – 21. Work out the rest of the message yourself.

The Telephone Call

I was mad and I was sad
and I was all upset,
I couldn't go outside to play,
the weather was too wet.

But then my best friend called me up
with lots of things to say,
we made each other giggle,
I felt better right away.

When you can't think of things to do
and the rain won't ever end,
it's nice to have a telephone
to share things with your friend.

by Jack Prelutsky

MEET
Peggy Rathmann

Peggy Rathmann was taking a class to learn about writing children's books when the idea for Ruby came to her. The class was told to imagine finding a piece of paper with something written on it.

Ms. Rathmann imagined a note passed between two girls that said, "You copied me! I'm telling!" because she kept wanting to copy other people's ideas. Peggy Rathmann says, "I drew Ruby to look like my little sister because I didn't want anyone to know the story was about me."

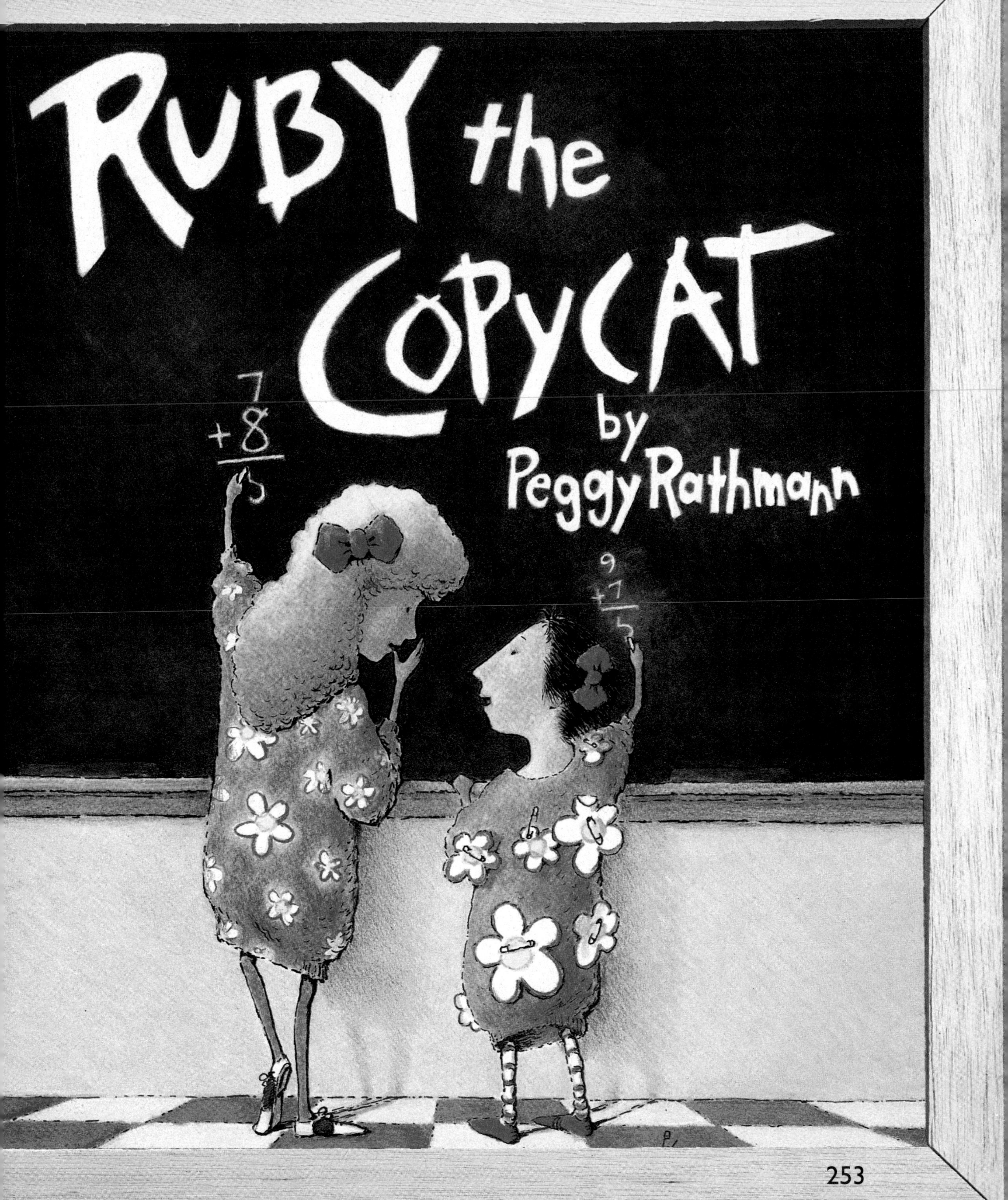
RUBY the COPYCAT
by
Peggy Rathmann
7
+8
5
9
+7
5

Monday was Ruby's first day in Miss Hart's class.

"Class, this is Ruby," announced Miss Hart. "Ruby, you may use the empty desk behind Angela. Angela is the girl with the pretty red bow in her hair."

Angela smiled at Ruby.

Ruby smiled at Angela's bow and tiptoed to her seat.

"I hope everyone had a pleasant weekend,"
said Miss Hart. "Does anyone have something
to share?"

"I was the flower girl at my sister's
wedding," said Angela.

"That's exciting," said Miss Hart.

Ruby raised her hand halfway. "I was the flower girl at my sister's wedding, too."

"What a coincidence!" said Miss Hart.

Angela turned and smiled at Ruby.

Ruby smiled at the top of Angela's head.

"Class, please take out your reading books," said Miss Hart.

At lunchtime, Ruby hopped all the way home on one foot.

When Ruby came back to school, she was wearing a red bow in her hair. She slid into her seat behind Angela.

"I like your bow," whispered Angela.

"I like yours, too," whispered Ruby.

"Class, please take out your math books," said Miss Hart.

On Tuesday morning, Angela wore a sweater with daisies on it.

At lunchtime, Ruby hopped home sideways.

When Ruby came back to school after
lunch, she was wearing a sweater with daisies
on it.

"I like your sweater," whispered Angela.

"I like yours, too," whispered Ruby.

On Wednesday, Angela wore a hand-painted
T-shirt with matching sneakers.

After lunch, Ruby hopped back to school
wearing a hand-painted T-shirt with matching
sneakers.

"Why are you sitting like that?" whispered
Angela.

"Wet paint," said Ruby.

On Thursday morning, during Sharing Time, Angela modeled the flower girl dress she wore at her sister's wedding.

Ruby modeled her flower girl dress, too, right after lunch.

Angela didn't whisper anything.

By coincidence, on Friday morning, both girls
wore red-and-lavender-striped dresses.
At lunchtime, Angela raced home.

When Angela came back to school,
she was wearing black.

On Friday afternoon, Miss Hart asked
everyone to write a short poem.

"Who would like to read first?" asked
Miss Hart.

Angela raised her hand. She stood by her desk
and read:

I had a cat I could not see,
Because it stayed in back of me.
It was a very loyal pet —
It's sad we never really met.

"That was very good!" said Miss Hart. "Now,
who's next?" Miss Hart looked around the room.
"Ruby?"

Ruby stood and recited slowly:

I had a nice pet,
Who I never met,
Because it always stayed behind me.
And I'm sure it was a cat, too.

Ruby smiled at the back of Angela's head.

Someone whispered. Ruby sat down.

"What a coincidence," murmured Miss Hart.

Angela scribbled something on a piece of paper. She passed it to Ruby.

The note said:

YOU COPIED ME!
I'M TELLING MISS HART!
P.S. I HATE YOUR HAIR THAT WAY.

Ruby buried her chin in the collar of her blouse. A big tear rolled down her nose and plopped onto the note.

When the bell rang, Miss Hart sent everyone home except Ruby.

Miss Hart closed the door of the schoolroom and sat on the edge of Ruby's desk.

"Ruby, dear," she said gently, "you don't need to copy everything Angela does. You can be anything you want to be, but be Ruby first. I like Ruby."

Miss Hart smiled at Ruby. Ruby smiled at
Miss Hart's beautiful, polished fingernails.
"Have a nice weekend," said Miss Hart.
"Have a nice weekend," said Ruby.

On Monday morning, Miss Hart said, "I hope everyone had a pleasant weekend. I did! I went to the opera." Miss Hart looked around the room. "Does anyone have something to share?"

Ruby waved her hand. Glued to every finger was a pink plastic fingernail.

"I went to the opera, too!" said Ruby.

"She did not!" whispered Angela.

Miss Hart folded her hands
and looked very serious.
"Ruby, dear," said Miss Hart
gently, "did you do anything
else this weekend?"

Ruby peeled off a fingernail.

"I hopped," said Ruby.

The class giggled.

Ruby's ears turned red.

"But I did! I hopped around the picnic table ten times!" Ruby looked around the room. "Watch!"

Ruby sprang from her desk.
She hopped forward.

She hopped backward.

She hopped sideways with
both eyes shut.

The class cheered and clapped their hands
to the beat of Ruby's feet. Ruby was the best
hopper they had ever seen.

Miss Hart turned on the tape player and said, "Follow the leader! Do the Ruby Hop!"

So Ruby led the class around the room, while everyone copied *her*.

And at noon, Ruby and Angela
hopped home for lunch.

Follow Me!

Ruby liked to hop. Think about things you enjoy doing. Choose a way to share your ideas.

- Pantomime something you like to do. Have the class guess what it is.
- Teach the class how to do something you enjoy.

The City Mouse and the Country Mouse

retold by Hal Ober

Characters

Flora, a country mouse   **Cricket,** a country cricket

Farrah, a city mouse   **Cat,** a city cat

Scene 1: *Evening, Flora's house, in the country*

Cricket: Flora! There's a lovely sunset tonight! Why are you inside, mousecleaning?

Flora: I have to, Cricket. My old friend Farrah is coming for a visit, and — *(There's a knock on the door.)* Oh, dear, that must be her. Just a minute! *(Flora opens the front door. In marches Farrah.)*

Farrah: I'm so exhausted! I must have walked for three hours through that field out there. I just hope I didn't get poison ivy.

Flora: Farrah! It's really you! It's been so long since we —

Farrah: Do you have anything to eat? I'm starving.

Flora: Of course! Sit down. I've made one of my favorite dishes for you. *(She sets down a plate.)*

Farrah: What's this?

Flora: Squashed acorns, wild oat seeds, and a buttercup of dew. Eat up!

Farrah: *(She tries a little and makes a face.)* Yuck! *(She pushes the plate away.)* What do you do for fun around here?

Flora: Well, I usually watch the sunset, read a book, and go to bed. But tonight I thought we might play a game of pick-up sticks!

Farrah: How totally thrilling. *(She yawns.)* What do you say we just go to sleep?

Flora: Of course! I've got your bed all ready.

Scene 2: *Inside Flora's bedroom*

Farrah: OUCH! What's in here, anyway?

Flora: *(Getting into bed)* Straw.

Farrah: Ugh. Feels as though I'm sleeping on shredded wheat. I just hope I can —

Cricket: Cricket Cricket. Cricket Cricket.

Farrah: WHAT ON EARTH IS THAT?

Flora: *(Waking up)* Huh? What's wrong?

Farrah: How can you sleep with that awful racket going on?

Flora: It's just Cricket saying his name. *(She snores softly.)*

Cricket: Cricket Cricket. Cricket Cricket.

Farrah: *(Burying her head under a pillow)* I give up!!

Scene 3: *Next morning, same place*

Flora: Good morning, Farrah! How did you sleep?

Farrah: I didn't.

Flora: Well, never mind, I've got a wonderful day planned. First we'll have a breakfast of toadstools —

Farrah: Listen, Flora, it's not your fault. But sleeping on straw and eating seeds and nuts in the middle of nowhere, well . . . it's just no life for a mouse!

Flora: It's not?

Farrah: No! And as your oldest and dearest friend, I've decided to show you what you're missing. We're going to the city!

Flora: We are?

Farrah: Come on. Out the door and don't look back!

285

Farrah: The movies! The museums! The food! I'm telling you, Flora, you'll love it here. And you'll forget you ever lived anywhere else.

Flora: *(A taxi screeches by them.)* Yikes!!!

Farrah: Look out for that shoe! Watch your tail! Okay, here's my mail slot. Follow me!

Scene 5: *In the living room of a fancy*
apartment, where Farrah and Flora are sitting
on a table surrounded by food

Farrah: Oh, they must have known we were coming! Hee-hee! Look at all the goodies! What did I tell you?

Flora: Are you sure it's okay?

Farrah: Of course it is. Hmmm, should I start with the roast turkey or the crackers and cheese? Maybe I'll eat dessert first and work my way back to the egg salad.

(Flora nervously sniffs a strawberry.)

Farrah: Makes your squashed acorns look a little boring.

Flora: It's all very nice, but —

Farrah: Oh! Try the cake!

Flora: Well, maybe just a nibble . . .

Cat: How is it?

Flora: Mmm! Delicious!

Cat: Oh, good.

Flora: *(She sees the cat.)* Oh, help! *(Farrah grabs Flora by the paw and snatches her away before the cat pounces.)*

Farrah: Hurry! Run for it!

Scene 6: *Inside Farrah's mouse hole*

Flora: I wanna go home! I wanna go home! I wanna go home!

Farrah: I think you'll be more comfortable IN the bed, not UNDER it.

Flora: *(Squeaking with fear)* That's okay! I'll stay here!

Farrah: Suit yourself.

Cat: Sleep tight, little mouseburgers. I'll see you in the morning!

Scene 7: *The next morning, inside Farrah's mouse hole*

Farrah: Good morning, Flora. I guess you didn't sleep well under the bed. But never mind, I've got a great day planned and — What's this? *(She reads a note left on a table.)*

Dear Farrah,
Thank you for showing me what I've been missing.

Yours truly,
Flora

Scene 8: *Flora's house in the country —
Cricket is sitting in the window*

Cricket: Flora! I knew you'd come back. How was the city?

Flora: It was interesting, Cricket. And I learned something very important.

Cricket: Oh? What?

Flora: It's better to feel safe with a little than to feel scared with a lot.

Cricket: I learned something, too.

Flora: What's that?

Cricket: A house just isn't a home without your best friend.

Flora: Aw, thanks, Cricket. There's a lovely sunset tonight. Shall we have a look?

Cricket: Let's. *(They go outside.)*

two friends

by Nikki Giovanni

lydia and shirley have

two pierced ears and

two bare ones

five pigtails

two pairs of sneakers

two berets

two smiles

one necklace

one bracelet

lots of stripes and

one good friendship

GLOSSARY

This glossary can help you find out the meanings of some of the words in this book. The meanings given are the meanings of the words as they are used in the book. Sometimes a second meaning is also given.

A

advertise To give out signs, posters, and other notices to the public: *Dillon put up posters at school to **advertise** his new babysitting business.*

angry Feeling very upset with someone: *Mrs. Jackson was **angry** when we broke her window.*

apartment One or more rooms used as a place to live. An apartment is in a building that has groups of rooms just like it.

apartment

B

bark **1.** The sound a dog makes. **2.** The skin of a tree. Bark is thick and tough. It covers the trunk and the branches.

bark

basement The lowest floor of a building, usually below ground: *Brian went down the steps to the **basement** to get some tools.*

blink To close and open the eyes quickly: *Tony **blinked** when he stepped out into the bright sunlight.*

business The work a person does to earn money: *Mr. Potter is in the **business** of selling houses.*

C

claw **1.** A sharp, curved nail on an animal's foot: *The bird held on to the branch with its **claws**.* **2.** Part of the arm of a shellfish or an insect that can grab things: *Will the lobster use its **claws** to catch that fish?*

coincidence Two things that happen at the same time that seem planned but have not been: *It was a **coincidence** that both boys wore the same costume to the party.*

copy To make or do something that is exactly like something else: *Annie **copied** her sister's drawing and even used the same colors.*

crate A large box made out of wood: *The oranges came packed in a **crate**.*

crate

crawl To move slowly on the hands and knees: *The baby **crawled** into the bedroom.*

crest The top of something: *The children climbed to the **crest** of the hill.*

curious Wanting to learn about something very much: *Roberto asks a lot of questions because he is **curious** about everything.*

D

discover   To learn or find out: *I **discover** new things about my baby sister every day.*

duck   To lower the head or body quickly: *Kathy **ducked** to keep from getting hit by the ball.*

dune   A hill of sand made by the wind: *The children ran down the sand **dunes** at the beach.*

dune

E

enemy   A person or an animal that wants to hurt another: *A bird is the **enemy** of a worm.*

F

ferocious   Very mean and dangerous: *A hungry lion can be a **ferocious** animal.*

flower girl   A young girl who carries the flowers in a wedding: *Rosa is going to be the **flower girl** at her cousin's wedding.*

frames   The part of a pair of eyeglasses that holds the lenses in place: *Lisa chose red **frames** for her new eyeglasses.*

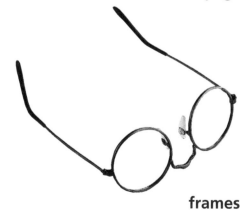

frames

G

ghost town A group of empty buildings that people no longer live in: *People used to work and live in Carson City long ago, but now it is a* **ghost town.**

H

hinge The part of a clam or an oyster shell that holds the two halves together: *A clam opens and closes its shell by a* **hinge.**

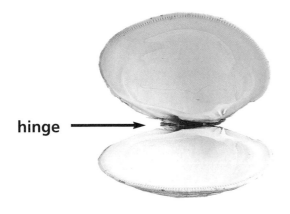

hinge →

hollow Having an empty space or a hole inside: *Some animals live in* **hollow** *logs or trees.*

hornet A large wasp that stings like a bee: *If a* **hornet** *stings you, it will hurt.*

hornet

I

imitation The act of copying the looks or sounds of something else: *Beth did a very funny* **imitation** *of a pig.*

J

jazz A kind of music: *They tapped their feet to the beat of the* **jazz** *music.*

295

K

kernel   A grain or a seed of a plant: *All the corn popped except for two* **kernels.**

L

learn   To get to know something by studying or practicing it: *I* **learned** *how to play the drums from my father.*

lenses   The parts of a pair of eyeglasses that help people see better by making things look clearer and less fuzzy. Lenses fit in a frame.

lighthouse   A tower with a strong light at the top that is used to guide ships away from dangerous shores: *The ship saw the* **lighthouse** *and sailed away from the rocky shore.*

lighthouse

loyal   Loving and faithful: *Tom is a* **loyal** *person who will do anything to help a friend.*

M

matching   To go well with: *Tina wore a sweater with* **matching** *slacks.*

model To show by wearing: *Joe* ***modeled*** *the new uniforms for the soccer team.*

murmur To speak in a soft, low voice: *The shy child* ***murmured*** *the answer.*

natural surroundings The place where an animal or a plant lives best or belongs. Crabs and oysters live by the oceans, which are their natural surroundings.

notice To see or hear something: *Look closely and you will* ***notice*** *the tiny lines on this leaf.*

opening A hole or clear space: *A turtle pulls its legs in through* ***openings*** *in its shell.*

opera A play in which most of the words are sung to music: *To play the part of the son in the* ***opera,*** *the young boy had to sing.*

opera singer

outgrow To grow too big for something: *The baby will* ***outgrow*** *her clothes quickly.*

297

P

pennant   A long flag, shaped like a triangle, that identifies a team: *Drew hung a basketball **pennant** on his wall.*

pennant

pod   The part of a plant that holds the seeds: *He had to open the **pod** to find the peas.*

pod

poke   To push forward: *My dog always **pokes** her head out the car window.*

polar bear   A large animal that has thick white fur and strong claws. Polar bears live in cold places.

polar bear

R

responsibility   Something that a person is responsible for: *My **responsibility** is to walk the dog every morning.*

responsible   Able to be counted on. A responsible person is someone you can trust to do a good job.

rickety   Likely to break or fall apart: *Mom will fix the **rickety** old chair so we can sit on it.*

rut A track in a dirt road made by wheels or feet: *The heavy truck left* **ruts** *in the road after the rain.*

S

scheduled A list of times when things are supposed to happen: *What's on the* **schedule** *for today?*

Saturday
9:00 Feed Buddy and Friskie
10:00 Go to playground
12:00 Eat lunch
2:30 Go to Ryan's house

shanty A cabin or shack that is falling apart: *The city is going to tear down the old* **shanties** *and put up new houses.*

shanty

share To let everyone have some: *Pedro enjoys* **sharing** *his toys with his friends.*

sharp Clear, not fuzzy: *My new camera takes* **sharp** *pictures.*

smooth Something that feels even and has no rough spots: *My baby sister's skin feels* **smooth.**

sneak To move in a quiet, secret way: *My dog* **sneaked** *onto the bed last night.*

soap opera A television show in which the story is continued from day to day. Soap operas got their name from the large number of soap commercials that were shown during the programs.

special Important and not like all the rest: *Birthdays are* **special** *days.*

spy   Someone who watches other people or things closely to get information about them. A nature spy is someone who looks closely at plants, animals, and other living things.

squint   To close the eyes partly to see better: *Jeffrey* **squinted** *at the words on the board.*

squint

storm   To move about in an angry way: *Ginny* **stormed** *into her room and slammed the door.*

straw   Stems of wheat, oats, or corn that are left after the seeds have been taken out. Straw is used as food for animals and for making hats and other things.

straw hat

suit of armor   Clothing made of metal. A long time ago, some people used armor to protect their bodies when they fought in wars.

suit of armor

300

T

teach To help someone learn: *Next summer, Mom will **teach** me how to swim.*

teller A person who works in a bank taking in and paying out money: *The bank **tellers** cashed a lot of checks today.*

tide-pool Water that remains in small holes in the ground after the tide goes out: *The sea gulls are feeding on the tiny fish left behind in the **tide-pools.***

tide-pool

track A set of rails that trains run on: *We heard the train coming down the **tracks.***

twilight The time just after the sun goes down, when there is still a little light in the sky: *The stars came out just after **twilight.***

W

windshield wiper A strip of rubber on a metal arm that goes back and forth over the window of a car to clear off rain and dirt: *Dad turned on the **windshield wipers** when it started to rain.*

ACKNOWLEDGMENTS

"A discovery!" by Yayû, from *Birds, Frogs and Moonlight,* haiku translated by Sylvia Cassedy and Kunihiro Suetake. Copyright © 1967 by Doubleday and Company. Reprinted by permission of Ellen Cassedy for the author.

Arthur's Pet Business, written and illustrated by Marc Brown. Copyright © 1990 by Marc Brown. Reprinted by permission of Little, Brown and Company.

"Build a Bug Home!" from *Superscience Red,* September 1994. Copyright © 1994 by Scholastic Inc. Reprinted by permission.

"Create a Funny Comic Strip," by Charles M. Schulz, from September 1994 *Disney Adventures* magazine. Copyright © 1994 by Disney Adventures. Reprinted by permission.

"Frog or Toad: How to Tell," from *The Complete Frog,* by Elizabeth A. Lacey. Copyright © 1989 by Elizabeth A. Lacey. Reprinted by permission of William Morrow & Company, Inc. Cover of March 1994 *Spider* magazine copyright © 1994 by Carus Publishing Company. Reprinted by permission of *Spider* magazine.

"Go on a Leaf Hunt!," from "Look What I Did with a Leaf!" from October 1994 *Child* magazine. Copyright © 1993 by Morteza E. Sohi. Reprinted by permission of Walker and Company, 435 Hudson Street, New York, NY, 1-800-289-2553. All rights reserved.

"The Goldfish," from *All Together,* by Dorothy Aldis. Copyright © 1925, 1952 by Dorothy Aldis. Reprinted by permission of G.P. Putnam's Sons.

"Hiding Place," by Nancy Dingman Watson, from *Secret Places,* selected by Charlotte Huck, illustrated by Lindsay Barrett George. Text copyright © 1993 by Nancy Dingman Watson. Reprinted by permission of the author. Illustrations copyright © 1993 by Lindsay Barrett George. Reprinted by permission of Greenwillow Books, a division of William Morrow & Company, Inc.

Julius, by Angela Johnson, illustrated by Dav Pilkey. Text copyright © 1993 by Angela Johnson. Illustrations copyright © 1993 by Dav Pilkey. Reprinted by permission of Orchard Books.

"Largest Pet Litters," from *Guinness Book of Records 1995.* Copyright © 1994 by Guinness Publishing Limited. Reprinted by permission.

"My Nature Journal," by Carolyn Duckworth. Copyright © 1994 by Carolyn Duckworth. Reprinted by permission of the author. Cover of July 1994 *Ranger Rick* magazine copyright © 1994 by The National Wildlife Federation. Reprinted by permission.

My Puppy, by Aileen Fisher. Copyright © 1953 by Aileen Fisher. Reprinted by permission of the author.

"Narrow Escape," from *KIND News Jr.,* October, 1990. Reprinted by permission of KIND *News.*

Nature Spy, by Shelley Rotner and Ken Kreisler. Text copyright © 1992 by Shelley Rotner and Ken Kreisler. Photographs copyright © 1992 by Shelley Rotner. Reprinted by permission of Macmillan Books for Young Readers, Simon & Schuster Children's Publishing Division.

"Parrot, Dog Are Honored at MSPCA Celebration," from *The Boston Globe,* May 6, 1988. Reprinted by permission of *The Boston Globe.*

"Parrot Honored for Saving Family," from *The Patriot Ledger,* May 5, 1988. Reprinted by permission of The Associated Press.

"Parrot Saves Family," by Eve Nagler, from July/August *U*S* Kids* magazine. Copyright © 1989 by Field Publications. Reprinted by permission of Children's Better Health Institute, Benjamin Franklin Literary & Medical Society, Inc., Indianapolis, IN.

"Parrot Wins 1988 Animal Hero Award," from *MSPCA Animal Action,* Winter 1988. Reprinted by permission of The Massachusetts Society for the Prevention of Cruelty to Animals.

"Pen Pals," by Beverly M. Lewis, from March 1993 *Highlights for Children.* Copyright © 1993 by Highlights for Children, Inc., Columbus, Ohio. Reprinted by permission.

"Project FeederWatch," by Cynthia Berger, from December 1992 *Ranger Rick* magazine. Copyright © 1992 by The National Wildlife Federation. Reprinted by permission.

Ruby the Copycat, written and illustrated by Peggy Rathmann. Copyright © 1991 by Margaret Rathmann. Reprinted by permission of Scholastic, Inc.

"Scuba Dog," by Virginia L. Russell, from June 1994 *Kid City* magazine. Copyright © 1994 by The Children's Television Workshop. Reprinted by permission.

Selection from *Secret Writing: Codes and Messages,* by Eugene Baker. Copyright © 1980 by The Child's World. Reprinted by permission.

"Taking Care of Biz," by Robert Price, from December 1993 *Ranger Rick* magazine. Copyright © 1993 The National Wildlife Federation. Reprinted by permission.

"The Telephone Call," from *Rainy Rainy Saturday,* by Jack Prelutsky. Copyright © 1980 by Jack Prelutsky. Reprinted by permission of William Morrow & Company, Inc.

"To Catch a Thief," from November 1993 *Ranger Rick* magazine. Copyright © 1993 by The National Wildlife Federation. Reprinted by permission.

"two friends," from *Spin a Soft Black Song,* by Nikki Giovanni. Text copyright © 1971, 1985 by Nikki Giovanni. Reprinted by permission of Farrar, Straus & Giroux, Inc.

Watch Out, Ronald Morgan!, by Patricia Reilly Giff, illustrated by Susanna Natti. Text copyright © 1985 by Patricia Reilly Giff. Illustrations copyright © 1985 by Susanna Natti. Reprinted by permission of Viking Penguin, a division of Penguin USA.

Peanuts "What a Drag!" from *Sunday's Fun Day, Charlie Brown,* by Charles M. Schulz. Copyright © 1962, 1963, 1964, 1965 by United Features Syndicate, Inc. Reprinted by permission.

What Kind of Baby-sitter Is This? by Dolores Johnson. Copyright © 1991 by Dolores Johnson. Reprinted by permission of Macmillan Books For Young Readers, Simon & Schuster Children's Publishing Division.

What Lives in a Shell? by Kathleen Weidner Zoehfeld, illustrated by Helen K. Davie. Text copyright © 1994 by Kathleen Weidner Zoehfeld. Illustrations copyright © 1994 by Helen K. Davie. Reprinted by permission of HarperCollins Publishers.

Where Does the Trail Lead? by Burton Albert, illustrated by Brian Pinkney. Text copyright © 1991 by Burton Albert. Illustrations copyright © 1991 by Brian Pinkney. Reprinted by permission of Simon & Schuster Children's Publishing Division.

Special thanks to the following teachers whose students' compositions appear in the Be a Writer features in this level: Sandi Abramson, Pine Grove Elementary School, Hood River, Oregon; Jacquelyn Peters and Kelly Valleli, Highland Elementary School, Charlotte, North Carolina; Kris Wroblewski, Valley View Elementary School, Las Cruces, New Mexico.

CREDITS

Illustration 17–50 Marc Brown; 61 Charles Schulz; 62–91 Dav Pilkey; 94–95 Ethan Long; 98 title by Artillery Studios; 115 Lindsay Barrett George; 116 title by Artillery Studios; 125–150 Helen K.Davie; 163–192 Brian Pinkney; 196–197 Elizabeth A. Lacey; 203 Susanna Natti; 204–222 Susanna Natti; 226 title by Artillery Studios; 231–246 Dolores Johnson; 251 JoLynn Alcorn; 253–280 Peggy Rathmann; 282–289 David Shaw; 290–291 Ed Martinez

Assignment Photography 52–53 (background), 125, 156 (b), 157 (tr), 159 (br), 160 (tl), 223, 227 (b), 251, 290–291 Banta Digital Group; 14–15, 16–17 (background), 18–19, 51 (background), 62–63 (background), 92 (background), 96–97 (background), 98–99, 114, 116–117 (background), 118–119 (background), 120–121, 122–123, 151, 152–153 (background), 154–155, 158 (tl), 159 (bl), 160–161 (background), 162–163 (background), 202–203 (background), 204, 224–225, 226–227 (background), 230–231 (background), 247, 252–253 (background), Tony Scarpetta; 16, 17 Alison Shaw; 12–13, 51 (inset), 92 (inset), 100–101, 121 (tr), 153 (insets), 193, 198–199, 200–201, 281 Tracey Wheeler

Photography 2 ©Tim W. Gallagher(t); 16 Alison Shaw/ Courtesy of Marc Brown(tl); 17 Alison Shaw/Courtesy of Marc Brown(br); 52 Courtesy of Kymbrly Ray; 54-55 Dwane L. Folsom(t)(m)(b); 54-55 R.B. Sanchez/The Stock Market(background); 56-57 ©Peter Steimer/The Stock Market(background); 56 AP Worldwide Photos, Inc.; 57 ©Peter Steimer/The Stock Market(background); 57 Courtesy of the Ascolillo Family(t)(b); 58 Chip Henderson/Tony Stone Images/Chicago Inc(bl); 58-59 ©Micheal Simpson/FPG International(t); 59 ©The Stock Market(br); 60 Gerry Gropp/Sipa Press(m); 62 Orchard Books(t); 62 Courtesy of Dav Pilkey(b); 93 Brian Seed /Tony Stone Images/Chicago Inc(tr); 93 ©Jeanne White/Photo Researchers(tm); 93 ©Browning Mary Eleanor/Photo Researchers(tr); 93 Patti Murray/Animals Animals(bl); 93 ©Richard L. Carlton/Photo Researchers(bm); 93 ©Tom McHugh/Photo Researchers(br); 96 Tim Davis(cover); 96 © 1990 Lawrence Migdale(tr); 97 © 1988 Lawrence Migdale(br); 102-103 Letraset; 102 ©Shelley Rotner(tl); 102 Courtesy of Ken Kreisler(br); 117 Gary Johnson(tr); 119 Stephen J. Krasemann/Photo Researchers(tr); 122 ©L. West/FPG International; 124 Courtesy of Kathleen Zoehfeld(t); 124 Courtesy of Helen Davie; 124-25 ©Randy Faris/Westlight; 152 Don Mason/The Stock Market(br); 153 Courtesy of Charles Helms(bl); 156-157 S.C. Fried/Photo Researchers(tl); 157 ©Tim W. Gallagher(bl); 157 Tom Walker (cover); 158-159 ©Tim W. Gallagher(t); 158 Stephen Krasemann/Photo Researchers(b); 159 Helen Williams/Photo Researchers(tl); 159 ©Tim W. Gallagher(mr); 160 ©Tim W. Gallagher(tl); 160 Photo Researchers(ml); 161 ©Tim W. Gallagher(tl); 161 Stephen Krasemann/Photo Researchers(mr); 162 Courtesy of Burton Albert(tl); 162 Courtesy of Brian Pinkney(bl); 162 Courtesy of Brian Pinkney(br); 194 John Gillmoure/The Stock Market(background); 197 Tom Walker(cover); 202 Courtesy of Patricia Reilly Giff; 203 Courtesy of Susanna Natti; 225 Courtesy of Jorge Hernandez; 226-27 Beverly Lewis; 228 Lee Stalsworth/Hirshhorn Museum(tr); 228 The Butler Institute of American Art(b); 229 Boston Athenaeum; 230 Courtesy of Dolores Johnson(tr); 230 Courtesy of Dolores Johnson(ml); 252 Courtesy of the McQuaid family(t); 252 Courtesy of Peggy Rathmann(b); 292 E. Bodin/Stock Boston(l); 292 Michael Melford/The Image Bank(r); 294 Tony Stone Images/Chicago Inc(l); 295 Animals Animals(r); 296 Harald Sund/The Image Bank; 297 Herb Snitzer/Stock Boston; 298 Joe Van Os/The Image Bank(tr); 299 Eric Neurath/Stock Boston(b); 300 Ron Slenzak/Westlight(br); 301 Steve Dunwell/The Image Bank